*Helping Vets Cope
with the Painful Legacy of
Combat Survival Skills*

WAR DAMAGE

BRINGING THE BATTLE HOME

Ted D. Kilpatrick Ph.D.

Former Lieutenant USNR

WAR DAMAGE: Bringing the Battle Home
Helping Vets Cope with the Painful Legacy of Combat Survival Skills

© 2019 Ted D. Kilpatrick Ph.D., All Rights Reserved.

Cover photo credits:
  © Shutterstock.com
    "Half Face portrait of Shell Shocked US Marine - Vietnam War" By John Gomez
    "Beautifully waving star and striped American flag" By sharpner

Book Interior Design / Cover Design by Suzanne Fyhrie Parrott

ISBN: 9781695460546 (paperback)

Printed in the United States of America

To the United States Warriors—those brave,
courageous women and men, past and present,
who have protected and preserved
our freedoms and independent way of life.

Introduction

I have used the terms "War-Damage" and "PTSD" (Post Traumatic Stress Disorder) interchangeably to describe symptoms experienced by many returning combat veterans. I prefer War-Damage instead of PTSD because, even though the civilian symptoms may be similar, returning veterans do not have mental health disorders so much as symptomatic "War-Damage." It seems inequitable to saddle them with a mental health label for something that combat stress caused while they were doing their duty.

PTSD now has a confusing connotation in the civilian world, often implying weakness, failure to adjust and a convenient road to legal action. Combat veterans do not typically use those justifications. Rather, the "War-Damage" symptoms veterans may experience are often from lingering "CSS" (Combat Survival Skills) they developed out of necessity while serving in a combat zone. Quick access to anger, readiness to fight, and constant alertness to danger are life-saving assets during combat.

This same dynamic generates guardedness in civilian life, limits our ability to make emotional commitments, and creates a tendency to be more comfortable in our own private world. Back home, it is expected that one is cautious responding to perceived threats, slow to anger, and available to emotional involvements. It is expected that you will be reasonably willing to share your personal life to facilitate social interaction. The nightmares, high startle reactions, emotional and physical distance experienced with loved ones, and social isolation commonly found in recently returned combat veterans are destructive to relationships and upsetting, but not necessarily a mental disorder. While many people understandably label those symptoms as PTSD, I prefer to define them as War-Damage to promote accuracy and provide deserved respect for veterans.

Those United States Warriors are historical and dedicated heroes who have secured our U.S. history, heritage, and example for all nations. They continue to prove that individual responsibility, honor, commitment, and contribution is the backbone of a great people.

Physical and emotional survival in a war zone require soldiers to redefine instinctive human values in order to kill unknown threats. This adjustment is more than just surviving. A war zone is unpredictable and dangerous at all times. Suspicion, distrust, stress, and anger become hardwired survival values. Your first response must be to fight. If you run or hide, you or your companions get killed.

This necessary internal rewiring builds a certain confidence and comfort level needed to inflict a fatal outcome for the enemy. This automatic response that is so valuable in a war zone is only corrosive to self and frightening to friends and family back home.

This is the War-Damage our nation required of our veterans, and it needs to be repaired before they return home and experience the confusing consequences that disrupts marriages, work, and friendships.

Acknowledgments

The many months it took to work on this book would not have been possible without the encouragement, support, and patience of my tolerant wife Carolyn White Kilpatrick. She was always at my side proofreading and helping to organize my memory and chapter sequences.

I also need to recognize the invaluable transcription services, corrections, and rough drafts prepared by my daughter, Diana Kilpatrick, a court reporter. A published author herself, she provided excellent advice on writing my own first book. My daughter Dana Kilpatrick added excellent suggestions to help explain the value of the book for War-Damaged veterans.

The technical advisor on South Vietnam combat locations and Marine fighting companies in I Corps was Major Dennis L. D'Arienzo, USMCR. He was invaluable in providing the Marine command structure, an understanding of jungle fighting, and descriptions of the demanding field conditions and stressful combat exposure leading to War-Damage.

A good friend and accomplished psychologist, Gerald E. Reynolds, Ph.D., who also has an undergraduate degree in English, provided expert editing. He corrected my sentence structure and inserted language for better readability. With his training and forty-plus years in practice, he also contributed valuable observations and offered professional input.

A successful author and computer expert, Leigh Edward Somers, mentored me throughout the long hours of writing and preparing the final manuscript. Without his dedication and expertise, I could not have finished.

Contents

Chapter 1
War Hurts Humans!

WAR-DAMAGE IS NOT A DISORDER. HOW DO I KNOW?

This book chronicles my thirteen months as a Navy psychologist during the early years of the Vietnam War (1966-1967). I served as ENS Kilpatrick, Division Psychologist near the demilitarized zone in I Corps, South Vietnam, while serving with the 3rd Marine Division near Da Nang and Phu Bai.

The combat fighting was intense during those years, and I saw about nine hundred psychological casualties with acute and chronic PTSD (Post Traumatic Stress Disorder). This allowed me firsthand knowledge of what caused PTSD for combat soldiers and the equally corrosive "War-Damage" to troops serving in an imminent danger war zone. I completed my tour but not without personal War-Damage scars. The same can happen to any of those enduring prolonged exposure to war zones, whether they're serving in the Marines, Army, Navy, Air Force, or Support Services. The overt PTSD symptoms of War-Damage have been well documented. The subtle causes and destructive impact of delayed or subclinical War-Damage is less understood and not as well documented. This book is about the less understood War-Damage our veterans may experience when they return home. Their subclinical injuries frequently show up later and have a long term and corrosive impact on their civilian lives.

I came home with such wounds and saw returning veterans suffering with similar effects while serving as the Navy psychologist at the Naval hospital in Jacksonville, Florida. Next, during thirty-five years in private practice, I worked with veterans who had similar concerns and symptoms of War-Damage. Like me, those veterans didn't admit they might have PTSD despite a destroyed marriage, ruined job opportunities, depression, and continued unhappiness. Therefore, they felt no need, inclination, or pressure to look for help until they became overwhelmed by alcohol abuse, drug addiction, or suicidal depression.

It has also been my honor to work with a few War-Damaged Marines during my retirement years. I provide consultation for them at no charge, which allows them to keep it private, without any public record, and without any detrimental diagnosis which would lead to loss of security status. We usually talk at breakfast, lunch, or by phone. We review their PTSD symptoms and personal relationships, and together we brainstorm their life ambitions. They talk easily to a former combat veteran, and over time we usually have a positive outcome.

From my own Vietnam experience and work with combat veterans, I learned the corrosive outcome of War-Damage that seems inevitable from serving in a combat zone. Most veterans come home without an opportunity to resolve their combat induced PTSD. Because Combat-Survival-Skills (**CSS**) have been rigorously drilled into them from their first day at boot camp through their entire time in military service, those returning veterans continue to carry those specific skills with them.

In a combat zone, veterans are always in a necessary "fight or flight" situation—an automatic reaction your central nervous system produces when you're in danger or believe you may be in danger. Even if you're scared to death the first time you're threatened, you have to adjust to controlling your nerves. In combat, running or hiding can get you killed. On the other hand, getting angry, facing threats, and fighting can save you and your buddies. .

This combat survival reaction saves lives time and time again. Thus, when veterans come home—still carrying those life-saving "combat-survival-skills"—they're constantly alert, anxious in unfamiliar and public places, and they're extremely guarded with loved ones, family, and friends. Seemingly in the blink of an eye, veterans can become explosively angry. They're unable to fully relax and enjoy being home. Some veterans express or attempt to deal with their lingering stress through excessive alcohol use, drug abuse, emotional isolation, social withdrawal, and intense flashes of anger.

Even though I was not involved in field combat situations at our division hospital, we were always in danger of attack by the enemy and we received incoming mortar rounds on a regular basis. We learned to be light sleepers so we could hear the mortars being fired, and we knew we had to get into our foxhole in six seconds or less, otherwise we might end up like raw hamburger if a mortar shell landed in our tent.

As one of the returning "War-Damaged" veterans, I was reluctant to discuss my combat experience and war trauma for years. I resisted initial opportunities for comfort from relationships with women. I needed their forgiveness and understanding to help resolve my, as yet unidentified, War-Damage and the carryover that impeded my civilian adjustment.

Instead, my combat zone PTSD left me with a poor sleep pattern, nightmares, anxiety, flashbacks, and guarded distance from any consoling attention. This response pattern, developed from long exposure to a combat zone, is not surprising since it arises from the basic instinct to survive, the combat training, and the war zone tension experienced for months at a time. I believe those responses become automatic and internally "hard-wired" in a very real sense and are typical of many, perhaps most, combat veterans.

Later, I did get married, but for years after my tour in Vietnam, I was known among friends as the "Quiet One." Whenever I went out to dinner with three close couples, I would sit for two hours and say little or nothing. As we left, I seldom shook hands or even said goodbye, despite having enjoyed the company, companionship, and conversation. Over time, my wife and good friends came to accept my behavior, and although it was known only to me, I remained lonely and confused about my interpersonal guardedness.

This "hardwired" survival adjustment, which is absolutely necessary in a combat zone, is nature's way of protecting us from the destructive daily stress of facing our own demise and having to justify killing frightened strangers. We must come to accept and value our "hardwired" personality adjustment to survive long term in a combat zone; otherwise, we would slowly come apart from the unrelenting fear and unknown dangers that can lead to ending up as a psychological war casualty. The huge challenge comes from the necessity of "rewiring" when combat veterans "return to the world."

This book chronicles my War-Damage recovery and the personal/professional insight I gained as I worked through the residual scars over many years. My recovery process made it possible to understand and work effectively with returning combat veterans. With this insight came my appreciation of the need for a program to address and treat the devastating and destructive effects of PTSD and War-Damage.

My final personal relief from lingering War-Damage came forty years after Vietnam following a life-threatening accident. The physical injuries left me temporarily crippled and in the hospital for three months. It took an additional six months for me to learn how to get out of bed, walk, talk and care for myself.

That devastating experience made me realize the value of sharing my feelings, fears, and need for interpersonal relationships with other people. They were all emotions I formerly kept in check because of my "hardwired" War-Damage. Fortunately, I was blessed to have a gentle, caring wife of thirty-five years who provided the "unconditional-positive-regard"—perhaps better known as "unconditional love"—that I needed to recover and gain insight into the way War-Damage had restricted my interpersonal relationships.

Before my accident, I was an athletic civilian and loved high-altitude mountaineering (McKinley in Alaska and Himalayan Mountains in Nepal). Then suddenly, I was a bedridden cripple. Because of this incomprehensible, overwhelming, and devastating accident that literally turned my life upside down, I became intensely suicidal (what I now label a "self-rescue-response") and was placed on a suicide watch while in the hospital. The title of my brief self-report (written during my accident recovery) says it all: "Death Without Dying." The daily depression and dependency of my prolonged accident recovery allowed me to "need" again.

I now find I can overtly express love for my wife and enjoy physical hugs from both men and women. The public anxiety and flashes of anger are finally gone, and I'm back to "living." I can now look forward to enjoying an enriched retirement. I don't recommend my "accident cure" as a treatment approach for lingering War-Damage/PTSD symptoms. However, the relief from those effects and the enriched interpersonal appreciation of friends and family are a comfort and joy. For years, my lingering War-Damage symptoms made me unnecessarily guarded and emotionally distant from those who cared for me.

Our brave women and men returning from combat zones may need similar support and relief from their military experiences. They have earned and deserve better treatment than being ignored after their dedicated service to our country. This book shares my experience with the causes of PTSD type symptoms for myself and most combat veterans. It also presents a viable remedy to minimize the lifelong impact of PTSD on newly "War-Damaged" veterans.

My approach recognizes the enormous value of working immediately with returning combat veterans. It's important to keep in mind that our military troops do not sign up for service with symptomatic PTSD. We spend millions of dollars for specialized training and more money to support our troops to fight and complete their combat role. Why not finish the job and resolve their "War-Damage" before they return to their loved ones? Our brave women and men can then prepare for and adjust to a comfortable civilian lifestyle. I propose a solution that should improve the civilian adjustment of combat veterans by working with them prior to their return home.

Ted D. Kilpatrick, Ph.D.
Former Lieutenant USNR

Chapter 2

TRAINING FOR A COMBAT ENVIRONMENT

It turned out, unknown to me at the time, that I'd acquired some good training for service in a demanding combat environment while growing up. My childhood exposed me to valuable outdoor experiences as a young boy of nine, ten, and eleven. We lived in rustic tent huts in the mountain foothills of the Tule River Indian Reservation near Sequoia National Forest above Porterville, California. My family had a logging company, and the most efficient way to get the logs from ten thousand feet on the mountain to the mill was to fell trees in the summer and put them on trucks to take them down to a lower elevation. The trucks carried full loads down the steep dirt roads to where the logs were cold-decked on the reservation at an altitude of thirty-five hundred feet. The logs would then be transported to the mill in Porterville, California, during the winter months.

We built our own wood huts with screened walls and a tin roof. We used outhouses and gathered our water from the river near the huts. My bedroom was on an outside wood porch that had 4x4 wood posts lodged in the edge of the river. It was my responsibility to maintain the outhouses, haul the water, and help work on the World War II trucks we used as logging trucks. It was all a valuable learning experience for a boy my age.

One of my early memories is straddling the water tank in the back of the cabin of my father's truck. I followed Dad's instructions as to when to turn the water on or off for the truck's water brakes. He was a wise man who instilled a good work ethic in me very early in life.

As an adult, I now know it was obvious that he could reach the water valve himself. But he made it seem as though it was the most important job on the truck on the steep descents we had to make from the upper levels of the mountain. Dad had built the upper dirt roads with Caterpillar bulldozers, and the roads were so steep, he used a Caterpillar chained behind the loaded trucks to slowly ease them down the steep stretches of road. Since I was out of school during the summers when we could get the trucks up to a high altitude, I spent every day proudly doing my duty turning on the water brakes to save the truck during the steep descents.

I also learned to grease the large wheel bearings by putting a glob of grease in my left palm and then slapping the wheel bearing into my palm while rotating it 360 degrees in all directions until the bearing was loaded with grease. This was another confirmation of being a valuable member of the logging team. Those daily chores fostered my self-confidence and my sense of worth and value.

By age ten, I was a tall, skinny kid. My lean arms became a valuable asset when a fully loaded truck broke off an axle in the bell housing between the wheels. This either required dumping the logs over the hill to repair the axle or jacking open the bell housing of the loaded truck. I could just get my small arm in the jacked-up bell housing and grab the end of the broken axle. My schoolteachers became used to my father showing up in hobnail boots, saying that he needed his son for an emergency truck repair.

I got out of school a few days every couple of months, and I was much appreciated by the loggers. They were able to save their load, and they could get their truck operational again after installing a new axle. My sense of worth and value was again enhanced, and I grew up a proud and confident young boy. I was comfortable with unknowns and proud of my ability to contribute when I was needed.

My outdoor experiences during those three years made me comfortable with my later duties as a navy officer supporting the Marines. The Tule Reservation had a herd of wild Mustangs part way up the mountain, and the chief of the reservation befriended me. He'd take me hiking through the woods to see the horses, and he also taught me a great deal about the forest plants and animals. I became extremely fond of Native American Indians.

I didn't begrudge my three-mile hike on a dirt road to catch the school bus each morning. I discovered that it was slightly shorter crossing a rattlesnake-infested hill to get to the bus stop, so that soon became my preferred route. I became an excellent shot with my slingshot and marbles and was able to fire a marble at the snakes and convince them to back away so I could safely transit the mountain. My father upgraded my ammunition by furnishing worn-out steel ball bearings that actually allowed me to knock a few rattlesnakes off their perch.

We had to travel twenty miles by buses to the Porterville school, and since I lived on the Indian reservation, I was originally assigned to the Indian school. After about a month in the fourth grade at the Indian school, the teachers came to my mother and suggested she move me to the "white" school, as I was too advanced for the fourth grade at the Indian school. This allowed me to learn a great deal about prejudice.

At the white school I was referred to as "Indian Lover" and was often harassed as I waited on an isolated corner of the white school for the well-labeled Indian bus from the reservation to pick me up. The older students took advantage of those opportunities to push me around, knock my books to the ground, and scatter my papers. The result of their prejudice was that I developed a great deal of respect and appreciation for Native American Indians. .

One day, as the older white boys were scattering my books and papers, the Indian bus arrived early. The Indian girls got off the bus and "cleaned house." They didn't really hurt the white boys, other than to knock a few down, but they darn sure scared the devil out of them. They made them pick up my books and papers and alerted the older white boys that they had better "leave Ted alone." I never had another problem with prejudice or harassment from the white students.

During the spring of our third year on the reservation, the chief came to me and told me to tell my father to leave our camp before dark and head for higher ground. He said the compound of our camp was going to be flooded because we were located in the old riverbed. We soon learned the hard way that there was a reason why nobody else wanted to utilize that nice level location—it was prone to flooding. I asked the chief how he knew a flood was coming, and he said that the frogs and turtles were all suddenly leaving the river for higher ground.

My father ignored the warning, and about 1:00 a.m. the next morning, he had to put all of us children on top of our large ice chest. He got his brother to help him carry the chest through waist-deep water, with us on top, to higher ground. That was the end of our logging compound on the reservation.

Fortunately, the stacked logs were piled at a higher elevation, and we could haul them into the mill that summer. By then, we had felled most of the timber at the higher elevations, so Dad made the decision to shut down the logging company, and we moved to

Visalia, California, to be near the rest of our family. The majority of our family had migrated with Mom and Dad to Visalia from Oklahoma during the Great Depression.

Dad bought an old warehouse with a big exhaust fan in the southern eave of the building, and it was there he built a roller-skating rink. I was recruited to help install the wooden floor and shelves for the rental skates. I worked each evening as a "whistle boy," helping to control the fast skaters and kids who might endanger other guests. I had to learn to be firm, but diplomatic, in order to control—without aggravating—paying customers or the parents of the younger skaters. That experience turned out to be excellent training for later in life when I had to deal with angry Marines in Vietnam.

The skating rink made for an unpleasant lifestyle as it involved working every night and every weekend. Dad eventually sold the rink and started a vending machine company, installing automatic coffee machines in local businesses and at the Port Authority of Stockton, California. We had several service trucks, and my job was to make simple syrup for the coffee machines out of sugar and hot water by rolling the syrup in gallon jugs on the floor. I also helped to service the coffee machines by arising before school to carry the paper cups, supplies, and small change necessary to resupply the vending machines. I usually rode with my dad, but sometimes rode shotgun with my grandmother, who drove to service shorter routes before my school.

I grew to be independent, self-sufficient, and proud that I could contribute to my family. My early work ethic was solidified, and at age fifteen, I moved away from my good but crowded home. I lived with a company-employed cousin at the coffee company service building, where we shared a small one-bedroom apartment at the back of the building. I continued to make good grades and played on the high school basketball team.

My religious parents took us to church every Wednesday evening and twice on Sundays. At some point, I started to lead singing (no instruments were allowed), and I was eventually preaching some on Wednesday evenings. By age sixteen, I was working on my grandfather's pig farm in Oregon feeding hogs, driving a tractor, and filling siphons to water our corn and maize crops. I was already tall at 6 feet 3½ inches and eating my grandmother's hearty breakfast of six eggs, bacon, toast, and potatoes—all fit for a growing boy in his teens. Good food supported my fast growth to approximately 175 pounds. My grandmother typically prepared large suppers and fed everyone else in the family first. She then gave me the remainder of the supper for my meal with a regular comment aside that I was "eating her out of house and home."

In mid-summer, I turned seventeen, and a college recruiter came by the Oregon farm from a new junior college starting up in Idaho. He found out I'd played high school basketball and invited me to attend the college that fall to play on their startup basketball team. The recruiter must have assumed I'd already graduated from high school, but in reality, I still had my senior year to go. Instead of finishing high school, I attended Magic Valley Christian College in Albion, Idaho. The small town (formerly called "Hang Town") was at thirty-seven hundred feet in rugged mountains between Idaho and Utah.

I did well in basketball and made good grades, but I needed money for food and expenses. I found a small church where I could preach on Sundays, still go to school full time, and practice basketball during the week. The church was located in the town of Burley, Idaho, about eighteen miles down the mountain from the school. On many Sundays I had to walk both ways. In the wintertime, a generous member of the congregation usually drove me back to school. My living expenses were covered by the combination of what I made preaching and what my basketball scholarship offered.

Eventually, the college kept asking for the high school diploma I didn't have. About Christmas time, I "fessed up" and told them that I'd skipped my senior year to attend their college. The college administrators were calm about it, as I was playing on the basketball team and had As in my first quarter in college. They also had a charter to start a high school, as yet unused. To solve both our problems, I became their first high school graduate. Needless to say, I didn't ever need to attend a prom or have to return for a ten- or twenty-year class reunion to see if I could still recognize aged high school classmates!

I met my first wife my freshman year in college and married her between my freshman and sophomore years. I was seventeen. My parents had to send written permission to Reno, Nevada, by bus, that summer as I would not turn eighteen for a few more weeks. We called the Marriage Office on our way from Oregon back to California. They remained open after 9:00 p.m. to wait for our arrival from the bus station with my parents' signatures. We got the license and married the next day at the local chapel. The marriage lasted only five years, until I finished my master's degree, but I have two beautiful, brilliant daughters (Dana and Diana), who are my pride and joy.

I transferred in 1959 to George Pepperdine University in Southern California. I was not tall enough or good enough to play basketball, but I did get an academic scholarship to help pay for books and tuition. My folks helped as best as they could, but I also worked two to three jobs during the evenings and on weekends. I preached at a local church that supplied a house and a small income for my family. I graduated Valedictorian of my bachelor's class with an undergraduate degree in psychology. That set me up for a scholarship to graduate school for a master's degree to pursue my interest in psychology.

Based on my college degree, I was able to find a full-time job as a probation officer for Los Angeles County. The job required me to work Fridays, Saturdays, and Sundays in a residential setting in the mountains with jailed delinquents. I had to stay overnight at the unfenced compound in the mountains on Friday and Saturday nights each weekend. We had a total of just four staff members, including me, to control the hundred-inmate population. We supplemented our staff with resident delinquents by giving them honored positions as "mayors, cooks, dorm monitors, runaway staff," etc.

I learned a great deal about group therapy and crisis management with those boys, as they injured or ran off arrogant or demanding staff in short order. The full-time income I earned in three days during the weekend let me focus Mondays through Thursdays on graduate school. I completed a two-year, sixty-hour master's degree and internship at the college's mental health clinic. My extended master's degree in psychology and mental health clinic internship qualified me for a direct commission in the Navy as a psychologist. My school deferments expired in the summer of 1965, and at age twenty-four (after receiving draft orders from my low draft number), I acquired a direct commission in the Navy Reserves.

All of my childhood and young adult experiences prepared me extremely well for the rigors of serving in a Marine field hospital in the northern part of South Vietnam. The Marines are a frugal service, and we had screened huts, cold showers, and basic meals. One night the enemy mortared our ammunition dump and almost all our ammunition blew up in our compound. That became a crucial resupply concern, because without ammo, we were much more vulnerable to enemy attack. For the next several days, all of the incoming planes carried ammunition rather than food or supplies for the deployed troops.

Fortunately, as the administrative officer for our officer's club (a converted shower which worked in reverse during the monsoon season), I had access to booze to replace my meager food rations. Three fingers of booze in a canteen cup (canteens cups hold nearly a quart of water), along with a couple of wormy biscuits, became my rations for a few days. I never begrudged the combat necessity to resupply the ammo compound. I understood that it was far better to have mortars, rockets, and ammunition to return fire rather than run the risk of having the NVA (North Vietnamese Army) overrun our compound.

To be trained for assignment to a combat zone in Vietnam, I was sent for thirty days to Camp Pendleton Marine Base in Southern California. The base was setup to partially mimic the Vietnam combat conditions with hidden spider holes, dense vegetation, and difficult terrain. I was assigned as part of a platoon of thirteen medical doctors who had also received orders for Vietnam. We were housed in open Marine barracks, issued camouflage clothing, and assigned a Marine sergeant (known as a "gunny sergeant") to put us through our pre-deployment training.

On our field march, we were provided with sleeping bags and backpacks to carry our gear. We were advised on that first day that we would hike approximately four miles into the California foothills. That was a comfortable assignment for me, but four of our medical doctors decided they didn't enjoy hiking with a backpack. Early in the hike, they returned to the barracks and followed the rest of us in their Cadillac. Their comment when asked about this behavior was, "What are they going to do? Send us to Vietnam?"

Since they were well aware of their Vietnam orders, the officers were somewhat disrespectful of the gunny sergeant, and they continued to drag their feet and delay following orders as much as they could get away with. When we were in the foothills setting up camp, I noticed the same four officers were cutting up small brush to prepare a comfortable bed for their sleeping bags.

I approached the gunny sergeant and asked if he saw what they were doing, and he replied, "Yes, Sir!"

I stared at him for a second and then said, "You're not going to tell them, are you?"

The gunny sergeant smiled. "No, Sir!"

The naïve, city-raised medical doctors had selected poison oak bushes to prepare their bedding. All four of them ended up in the hospital for several days suffering from a nasty case of poison oak. That was my initial experience learning the Marine Corps code of respecting the requirement to "Take care of yourself and be responsible for knowing what to do."

Since I had been shooting a rifle for much of my childhood, I did reasonably well on the rifle range with my M14. On the range, the gunny walked behind us with a scope, spotting and checking the accuracy of our shooting. At one point he came up to me and said, "Sir, you're about the only one to consistently hit the target." He then asked me to help supervise the other naïve officers who knew very little about shooting or handling a weapon safely next to other personnel. I learned a valuable lesson about respecting the chain of command, and particularly, the value of staff sergeants and gunny sergeants in the Marine Corps.

We were required to set up night ambushes while watching for "spider holes" full of Marines acting as the enemy. They would suddenly appear from below ground and fire blank cartridges our way to let us know we'd missed the "spider hole" and were therefore "dead." We also learned to climb Navy rope ladders in case we were ever on ships, and then we would jump from the bottom of the ladder and practice a parachute landing roll to be prepared to bail out of choppers.

The value of the Marine culture is to understand the sophistication of a shared defense where everyone is a fighter. The buddy system made us responsible for the care of our Marine companions in terms of fighting, protection, and if necessary, recovery. It is the code of the Marines to never leave another Marine behind. I did not fully appreciate the value of that training until our compound was probed one night in Phu Bai, Vietnam. Rather than just retreating in fear during the attack, the training kicked in, and I found myself engaged in the defense of the compound.

My start with the Navy came as a direct commissioned officer reporting to Bethesda Naval Hospital in Washington, D.C. in the fall of 1965. I was assigned for three months of orientation to learn how to salute and adjust to Navy procedures and properly wear the uniform. I was part of a fourteen-man platoon of other naval officers who had also received direct commissions. Most of them were M.D.s who came in as full lieutenants because of their medical training and experience. I was low man on the totem pole as a psychologist, so I entered as a fresh ensign, two ranks below lieutenant. As a psychologist, I was part of the Navy Medical Service Corps rather than the United States Navy Medical Corps.

We spent our mornings in close order drills with a staff sergeant. All fourteen members of my platoon took a turn at leading the rest of us neophytes as we attempted to march in uniform with military precision. When any one of us was leading the platoon (we were a group of rebels), we delighted in marching the platoon into the hedges surrounding the commanding officer's quarters. The staff sergeant tolerated this, despite frequent swearing, and even seemed to value our behavior as legitimate military rebellion.

One evening, I strained my right knee while showing off my dancing skills with a nurse at the Bachelor's Quarters. That injury necessitated me walking on crutches for a couple of weeks, which plunged me into a comedy routine every time I met a senior officer on the sidewalk. I had to tackle the unwieldy combination of moving my crutches to my left side while standing on my left leg and then saluting with my right hand. After a while, I met an admiral on the sidewalk, and as I went through my comedy routine to salute him, he paused briefly and returned my salute. He accurately perceived that I was one of the recent direct commissioned officers and assured me I didn't need to salute officers while I was using crutches. He told me that a brief nod of the head while in uniform and outside a building would suffice. That thoughtful officer made my life much simpler and taught me a lesson about respect and common sense in the Navy.

Our three months of orientation at Bethesda Naval Hospital was geared toward helping the Navy evaluate our skills and leadership potential in order to decide on our next duty station. We could be assigned to general duties in our field or given independent duty as the head of a department. I was fortunate to receive independent duty and reported to the large Norfolk Naval Hospital in Virginia as staff psychologist for that hospital.

I was there approximately a year and had an opportunity to work with Navy wives who were experiencing adjustment problems as their husbands left for six to nine months of sea duty. I also worked with several women who had experienced sexual abuse as children or physical assault as adults. My internship and degree in psychology had prepared me for working with these women using deep relaxation techniques in order to recall and resolve repressed trauma. I was soon an accepted member of the Norfolk Naval Hospital Staff. When I got my orders to "ship out" to Vietnam, a couple of doctors came to me and expressed concern that they were losing an important member of their team. They were suspicious of the war and chagrined to learn that the individuals they considered the "best and brightest" in the Navy were being assigned to Vietnam.

Chapter 3

ARRIVAL IN VIETNAM

I found myself jammed in with a couple of hundred grim-faced Marines, in rough battle dress, on a chartered Braniff Airlines 707. We were headed from Okinawa to Da Nang in South Vietnam. I left the U.S.A. in 1966 with good government/civilian support and public appreciation for our willingness to fight. We were going to confront the communist aggression of North Vietnam and its threat to take over non-communist South Vietnam.

The attractive flight attendants were most attentive and tolerant of the catcalls from the young Marines who were eager to make contact or just get some attention. We'd left in daylight, but by the time we reached Vietnam it was dark, and I could see no obvious evidence of an airfield. The pilots had communicated very little during the trip other than to give airspeed, altitude, and an estimated time of arrival. We descended to ten thousand feet, according to the pilot, and were reminded to fasten our seatbelt in preparation for landing.

As we crossed from ocean to land (in military jargon going from "feet-wet" to "feet-dry"), there were a few scattered lights on the ground but nothing that indicated the presence of an airport. After a brief interval of level flight at ten thousand feet, the pilot cut power and started a hard forty-five-degree left turn, circling while rapidly descending at a steep angle. Suddenly, lights came on indicating an airstrip. The pilot continued his circling descent, and then at a fairly low altitude, he quickly lined up the 707 with the airstrip.

There were occasional flashes of light a few miles distant from the airstrip that I later learned were parachute flares. They were used as a security measure to help Marines on the ground identify enemy contact and discourage the enemy from getting too close if they neared the perimeter wire or the airport's defensive positions.

I also later learned that the pilot's seemingly unorthodox approach, known as a "military approach," was designed to keep the airplane over the airport in a rapid descent for landing. This minimized the possibility of ground fire from the enemy while we were landing. It must have worked well, as we completed our landing and stopped quickly with reverse thrust on the engines and brakes on the landing gear.

We proceeded to taxi off the landing strip, and the landing lights were quickly extinguished. The pilot proceeded to follow a dimly lit Jeep to an equally dimly lit area where the receiving Marines were standing at full attention on the door side of our aircraft. The stewardesses disappeared while the Marines gathered their duffle bags and quickly disembarked from the aircraft. The Marines were directed by the receiving Marines to locations away from the aircraft where their paperwork was reviewed for appropriate assignments.

As I exited the aircraft with a couple of other Marine Corps officers, the "Fog of War" quickly overwhelmed me. My orders as a Navy psychologist (not a Marine officer) did not seem to fit in with the Marine Corps preparations for individuals with my specific orders. I was directed to stand away from the bulk of the Marines and told to sit down on my duffle and wait.

I soon found myself completely alone as the other Marines moved away to housing, transportation, or the units to which they were assigned. After about forty-five minutes, a Jeep showed up with darkened headlights, and I was ordered into the back seat. I was transported to a small hut on the edge of the airstrip and again told to sit down and wait while my paperwork was reviewed.

Evidently, there were no pending orders for my arrival, nor any standard orders for what the Marines were supposed to do with me. (I later learned I was unexpected, as I had arrived prematurely since the Navy psychologist I was replacing had been evacuated as a psychological causality.) Eventually, after midnight, two heavily armored Jeeps showed up with mounted machine guns and armed Marines in the seats and two manning the machine guns. I was directed to the back seat of the second Jeep.

We sped out into the dark night without headlights and transitioned from a paved road to a rough and poorly maintained secondary dirt road. We sped around "Monkey Mountain" (a place of intense fighting when the Marines first arrived) on our left and passed several darkened compounds before turning into a separate facility with small hospital signs on some of the buildings. The Marines in my Jeep asked me to exit the vehicle and motioned me toward a small, darkened wood hut. The Jeeps immediately reversed direction and left the compound at a high rate of speed, and I found the small hut locked and no one available for support or direction.

I waited by myself for a while, and then out of impatience, I started to wander around the wooden framed buildings with screened walls and tin roofs. Initially, I had no luck but ultimately found one building with people talking inside. Several Marines were engaged in a friendly game of poker. I introduced myself to the men at the table and asked directions to the command facilities. I was informed that such facilities were not available at that time of night.

Finally, one of the gunnery sergeants took pity on me, interrupted his poker game, and asked to examine my orders. After glancing through my papers, he suggested I follow him, and he led me to another wood framed building where he opened the screen door and indicated an empty bunk. He suggested I crash for the night and informed me that breakfast was served from 6:00 a.m. to 8:00 a.m. Then the mess tent closed.

That first night in Da Nang I lay down in my marine fatigues and got a little sleep. The rustle of other troops in the tent awakened me at about 6:00 a.m. I got directions to the mess tent and managed breakfast, despite being totally out of place in my clean fatigues and starched Marine Corps cover (officer's cap). I figured out which tables housed the officers, primarily by observing their cleaner degree of dress as compared to other Marines in the tent who looked like they needed a shower and their clothes laundered, which they did based on their defensive duties.

A kind soul helped me out and directed me to the Command facilities where I showed up promptly at 7:00 a.m. Once again, I found no one home and no instructions as to how I should proceed. I returned to my temporary bunk and slept briefly until another officer noticed my presence and began to ask relevant questions as to my Marine assignment and anticipated duties. When he found out I was a Navy ensign assigned as division psychologist to the 3rd Marine Division, he smiled knowingly and suggested I follow him. He led me to a nearby wooden structure and shared my orders with an officer who turned out to be a Navy lieutenant commander serving as division psychiatrist for the 3rd Marine Division.

The psychiatrist was a friendly, relaxed, and accommodating officer who indicated he was very glad to see me since they'd lost their previous division psychologist as a psychological casualty. The lieutenant commander had been carrying the load of all the referred combat Marines and was pleased to have my additional help. He walked me to the now staffed Command Operations Center (COC) where I submitted my orders, which immediately generated significant confusion. The division psychiatrist remained with me while the Marines in the COC indicated I was at the wrong place and should have reported to Phu Bai in Northern I Corps. This was the new location for the medical compound supporting the 3rd Marine Division. It was suggested that I stand by for a chopper ride north to check in at my assigned duty station.

The knowledgeable psychiatrist came to my rescue and indicated it was a little silly to put me on a chopper over enemy territory only to honor the paperwork before returning me to Da Nang to start work as the division psychologist. He obviously knew how to work the system, and with his rank and his need for my help, he won the argument. I was informed that without going to Phu Bai, my paperwork could not be completed, and therefore I would not receive any income, combat pay, etc. That would continue until the paperwork was officially received, cleared, and I was assigned to the appropriate duty station.

This That was fine with my friendly psychiatrist, who was primarily looking for additional help. We were receiving a lot of combat Marines who needed evaluation, treatment, or evacuation for their combat War-Damage. When the psychiatrist won the argument, I was assigned a permanent cot in one of the officer huts. I walked to the hut to get squared away and was told to return for duty by 10:00 a.m. that same morning to help evaluate combat casualties.

I still felt like a fish out of water, but that sequence of events turned out to be a real blessing in disguise. The psychiatrist had been "in country" for about nine months, had learned his duties well, and was a talented medical professional. He let me observe his evaluation process for psychological combat injuries and then gave me the blessing of a debriefing on my initial attempts evaluating Marines with similar War-Damage.

Our options on treating those injured Marines were quite limited. We had a ten-bed ward where we could treat Marines for a few days, we could evacuate them offshore to hospital ships, reassign them to rear area duties, or evacuate them out of the country. My initial inclination was to keep most of them in country, but I found this was impossible when we were getting hit hard with dozens of combat casualties over a few days. I learned the necessity of compromise and settling for a less than ideal decision in order to keep psychological casualties moving through the system.

I had a crash course in evaluating War-Damage (PTSD). I was surprised to find that I was totally wrong about my naïve assumption that individuals would be malingering or faking combat stress to get off the front lines. The young Marines I saw were legitimate psychological casualties, and in the thirteen months I spent as division psychologist, I can count on one hand those individuals I thought were just pretending to be ill or trying to get away from the discomfort and stress of duty with their combat unit. Marines are very loyal to their unit and buddies, and malingering is not part of the Marine culture.

One evening, shortly after I arrived, the psychiatrist came to my hut and asked that I follow him to see something not often observed. He led me to the perimeter guarded by Marines, barbed wire, personnel mines, etc. We soon stood outside an enlarged fighting hole designed for defense and protection from mortar attacks. The hole was approximately eight feet long, four feet wide and five feet deep. Inside the foxhole stood a single Marine with an M14 rifle and a no-nonsense warning not to approach.

The talented psychiatrist backed off and soon had him talking. It became obvious that the young Marine was having trouble communicating and expressing himself in a coherent fashion. Ultimately, the psychiatrist talked him into laying down his M14 rifle and relaxing on a chair the psychiatrist had brought to the fighting hole. There was no suitable place to sit down since four to six inches of water filled the bottom of the hole.

No obvious external injury was visible, but the Marine was certainly hurting. The psychiatrist provided cigarettes, matches, water, hot drinks, cheese, sandwiches, and some sort of pudding on a serving tray. The brilliance of that approach soon allowed the psychiatrist to talk the young Marine out of the foxhole while still retaining his weapon. *Marines are taught from day one to never lose their weapons nor leave their weapons behind.* The next day the young Marine was evacuated to a full hospital in Japan. During the debriefing, the psychiatrist educated me on spotting and addressing traumatic brain injury (TBI) that can result from a nearby explosion.

That experience and education served me well a few months later when I was called to our perimeter at the 3rd Medical Division in Phu Bai. I needed to decompress a Marine who had already shot his M14 at approaching Marines attempting to confront him. He was threatening to shoot anyone who came close and had shot away a small pine tree near the last person who had attempted to talk to him. In desperation, the commanding officer of the medical battalion asked me to help.

I practiced what I'd learned from my psychiatrist mentor and didn't approach this Marine without a lot of verbal warning as to my location and my desire to be helpful. I ordered cigarettes, snacks, coffee, etc., to be delivered to me so I could transfer them to the location of the agitated Marine. I honored his request for a jacket and added a folding chair that he could use to be more comfortable.

After an hour of getting to know him with questions regarding his family and stateside experience (what we called "back in the world"), he began to accept that I was not a threat. I was being honest and predictable when I told him that he was in charge and I would do as he requested. He ordered a couple of armed Marines to move farther away and seemed reassured and more relaxed when I supported his request for the Marines to back out of sight. You have to understand that Marines are action-oriented individuals. They're brave and would not have hesitated to confront another armed Marine had it been necessary to do so.

After an hour, I was able to get the agitated Marine to follow me back to my small wooden office while still shouldering his M14 rifle. I alerted him ahead of time that my corpsman would ask for his rifle, as we didn't allow combat troops to enter my hut with weapons. That led to a small crisis when we were ready to enter my office, but the Marine did let me have the weapon, and I was able to transfer it to my corpsman before the Marine sat down across from me.

This Marine had also experienced near-proximity to significant explosions and was obviously experiencing traumatic brain injury (TBI). Without the experience and education I'd received early in my Vietnam assignment from the savvy psychiatrist, I would probably have totally screwed up this situation. I evacuated the young man the next day to a hospital in Japan, since sending him to a hospital ship offshore was not going to resolve his issues.

The one occasion of malingering that stands out in my mind came about mid-tour during the "winter" months in northern South Vietnam. The medical compound in Phu Bai was near Hue, which is close to the southern edge of the DMZ (demilitarized zone). Although it's above freezing all year, forty-degree rainy weather is still cold, and the Marines I saw were often dressed in overcoats and warm clothing. The corpsmen were assigned to relieve them of weapons before letting them into my hut. My corpsman missed one of the Marines who had a .45 caliber weapon (pistol) under a coat in the back of his belt. He got through our screening and into my office. After hearing his concerns and reviewing the trauma he'd been through, it became obvious that he merely wanted to get away from the discomfort and threat of a combat environment.

After listening, I sympathized with his stress and indicated that I'd let him stay a few days in my ten-bed casualty ward and get some hot food and rest before returning him to his unit. There was a long pause while he stared at me with evil eyes before he casually reached behind his back, pulled out his loaded .45, and laid it on the desk with the barrel towards me. He casually asked me, in a no-nonsense voice, if I was sure about my diagnosis and treatment.

When faced with a Marine holding a loaded .45 pointed at you, it's really easy to adjust your game plan. I knew he was malingering, but nevertheless, I put him on an in-country plane that day from Phu Bai to Da Nang. As part of the deal, I guaranteed he was relieved of all weapons and escorted him personally to the plane that afternoon. After he was seated on the plane, I informed the pilots that I'd be contacting the military police, and they would be meeting the plane.

Since I knew he was malingering, and he had threatened me, I was understandably angry and looking for a little payback. It was not particularly mature of me, but I asked the military police to escort him to the brig in Da Nang and advised them that I would be by to evaluate and release him at a later date. His release date came months later when I had orders to return to "the world."

I was able to stop at the brig for a prolonged discussion with the Marine on my way home. He acknowledged my legitimate reason for upset and finally came clean that he hadn't been particularly stressed from combat but was just cold, tired, and faking his anxiety. Between his time in the bush and his time in the brig, he was still due for rotation, and we basically left the country together. I didn't feel any need to make additional difficulties for him, since his career as a Marine was probably over, and he no longer wanted to serve.

That's my only memory of being physically threatened with a weapon by a combat Marine. They're historically respectful of officers, and despite seeing young men in extreme psychological distress, I never felt threatened or concerned about retribution if I asked them to return to their unit or serve in a rear area until they were due for rotation. I became very loyal to Marines as I was exposed to the stresses those young men faced in many combat situations. They saw their best buddies killed right next to them, and often had to survive by their own wits, training, and courage.

My admiration and loyalty for those brave men may have caused me to be overly concerned or generous with some of my decisions. Overall, I became confident of my ability to evaluate the level of their stress and the potential destructiveness on the rest of their lives of continued War-Damage. When possible, I adjusted their location or combat duties to let healing begin.

My dedication to those young men got me in serious trouble with a marine corps general whose duties kept him in a rear area near our medical battalion. I had seen a Marine with about nine months of repetitive combat missions. During his time in the jungle, he'd lost many of his friends in combat. With experienced judgment, his local commander referred him for combat stress. I agreed with the commander's evaluation. The Marine had done his duty, and I felt that additional front-line combat could very well cause lingering War-Damage. I decided this would not well serve the Marine Corps or this brave Marine.

I assigned him to our area motor pool where he served as both a mechanic and driver. One day he drove a large Marine truck the wrong way down a dusty dirt road. That action put a lot of dust onto the general's office desk. The general was so angry, he found out who was driving the truck. Since the Marine was driving the wrong way on a clearly marked street and should have noticed that he wasn't allowed to proceed in that direction, the general was even more agitated.

The general immediately ordered him back to his front-line company in the bush. The young man came by to see me in his combat gear and thanked me for the support he'd received. He acknowledged his mistake on the general's road and informed me that he was returning to the bush. It was my professional judgment that he wasn't ready, and we'd be exposing him to significant additional stress that could very well result in a serious post-traumatic stress disorder.

I overrode the general's reassignment (without informing the general) and evacuated the young man back to "the world" that afternoon. I did this without clearing it with the general—a serious mistake on my part! Somehow, the general found out what had happened and who had been responsible for evacuating the Marine. He came down on me with a vengeance. He wrote up a negative fitness report, indicating that I was stupid, biased, disrespectful of command, etc. I'm sure he would have sent me to the bush with nothing but a pocketknife, if he'd been able to do so.

When my commanding officer received a copy of that fitness report, he wrote his own. He forwarded it to the general, indicating the contribution I'd made to the 3rd Marine Medical Division and described with complimentary terms my professional skills, intelligence, and combat experience in Vietnam. He further suggested I'd probably made a good decision. The general wouldn't let it go, and he wanted a report from me justifying my decision and acknowledging my bias and incompetence.

I did write the general a report indicating why I'd made my decision, and I suggested that "HE" would have been exposed to serious repercussions if he were the active reason a combat Marine experienced mental illness for the rest of his life. In my petulant way, I further acknowledged that I'd be happy to forward my report to Division Headquarters.

That ended the incident, but I was careful not to be caught in the vicinity of the general's compound. He was a Marine through and through, and I felt that he might very well have figured out how I could experience a serious "accident." Obviously, my paranoid concerns were out of line, and both the general and I got over our "disagreement." His outstanding credentials as a Marine Corps General and my commander's appreciation of my contribution as the division psychologist won the day. I have had no contact with the young Marine since Vietnam, but I'm reasonably confident that his courage and dedication to his duties as a Marine have probably stood him in good stead in the civilian world.

Chapter 4

THE MOVE TO PHU BAI

After about a month in the more secure area of Da Nang, I was ordered to my permanent duty station in Phu Bai, Vietnam. This was located well north of Da Nang, near the DMZ (demilitarized zone), and close to the former capitol of South Vietnam, called Hue. This was a much more remote facility with a large ammo dump and primitive military huts for Army and Marine troops plus a basic field hospital for the 3RD Marine Division.

The entire compound was enclosed inside a perimeter of barbed wire. Viet Cong and NVA (North Vietnamese Army) occasionally tested the compound at night by attacking with small arms and satchel charges. When successful at breaking into the compound, they'd throw their satchel charges into the tents and bunkers in an attempt to kill military personnel. The base was occasionally mortared, although the mortars were usually directed at the Marine housing or ammo dump rather than the field hospital.

In transitioning from Da Nang to Phu Bai, I had to make a couple of trips in large CH-53 helicopters—noisy transport aircraft that could carry a large number of Marines. On one occasion, as I returned from Phu Bai to Da Nang, we had a limited number of Marines on board. The pilot suddenly came on the intercom and indicated he had an engine warning and would have to make an emergency landing. The landing site was still in "Indian

Country" (enemy territory), and he settled the craft successfully near the base of a small hill. The set down was hard but certainly not a crash landing. The pilot was immediately on the intercom indicating he had an engine alarm that showed the engine had a sudden influx of metal particles and should be shut down.

I was wearing a .45 semiautomatic pistol at the time, whereas the Marines onboard had M14 rifles. I was handed an M14 by the chopper crew chief and directed to an area outside the aircraft with orders to be vigilant and to prepare for enemy action. He told me to find a depression or small hole and partially hide myself and be alert for enemy approach. That was my first clear reminder that everyone who serves with the Marines is still a combatant. I found a less than suitable spot and lay on my belly with my back to the aircraft. It was comforting that Marines were in prone positions to my right and left. We soon observed enemy troops coming down the hill.

They stopped abruptly when helicopters and gunships showed up to protect our aircraft. Obviously, the pilot had immediately called for backup, and the support Hueys brought in additional "grunts" (Marine infantry). The damaged helicopter was quite valuable, and mechanics immediately started to evaluate how serious the problem was and whether or not the aircraft could be flown out to Da Nang. I returned my M14 to the crew chief, was placed on a rescue helicopter, and then allowed to depart for Da Nang. Other Marines from the original helicopter and the back-up grunts began to dig fighting holes. I must say I have had little enthusiasm for helicopters ever since.

I did have to make a few more chopper flights to remote areas farther north and closer to the DMZ. Those trips were in response to the needs of battalion medical officers who had serious psychological casualties. On one of the helicopters, I noticed small bright holes in the side of the fuselage next to me. The crew chief informed me they were from small arms fire during a previous trip. I traveled safely in and out of those remote locations while helping the battalion surgeons. Nevertheless, I remained leery of the helicopter's mechanical ability and defensive strength to complete the journey.

I did learn to carry cigarettes with me, despite not being a smoker. The noise of those Vietnam era helicopters was so bad that we broke the filters off the cigarettes and stuffed the filters in our ears for hearing protection. The smokers onboard became quite popular just prior to takeoff. I learned to carry one or two packs in my pockets to pass out to the troops who weren't smokers or didn't have cigarettes to use for hearing protection.

Shortly after my arrival in Phu Bai, I was introduced to ground combat. In an effort to reach out to the locals, Marines visited adjacent villages with medical supplies. We treated the children with minor diseases or injuries and the adults for stomach problems, usually related to various worm conditions. The rules required that an officer be present with the platoons as they walked across the rice fields. If the fighting was more remote, we walked on the raised dirt levees designed to contain water in the fields. These were relatively dangerous missions, since the platoon was exposed and there was no guarantee we wouldn't come under enemy fire.

As the youngest officer in the field hospital, I was immediately assigned to fulfill the requirement that an officer accompany the platoon. The first morning that I showed up to accompany the platoon, I noticed that my fatigues were relatively clean and "Marine green." I also had on the traditional starched Marine cover, whereas the other Marines were in dirty, baggy fatigues, and wore "boonie hats." I was wearing a .45 pistol, and the rest of the Marines had M14 rifles. None of us wore insignia, but it was still obvious that I was probably the officer assigned to the platoon.

I approached the platoon sergeant in charge and asked him whether or not it was wise for me to stand out so obviously in my clean fatigues, packing my .45. His reply was, "No, Sir!" I asked whether he could help me, and he said, "Yes, Sir!" He left and shortly returned with dirty combat fatigues, a boonie hat, and an M14 rifle. He took my .45 and had me change clothes and boots to rid me of my shiny, stateside footgear. He assigned me a position in the middle of the platoon, and we walked fifteen feet apart to avoid having a single mortar round take everyone out. To describe me as nervous is a gross understatement, though I was greatly reassured by the seasoned combat Marines who obviously knew what they were doing. As we marched, I grew increasingly confident of their ability to defend themselves and me.

On one occasion, I was in the middle of a village applying an antibiotic ointment to a child's head lesion when rifle fire erupted. I gave the tube of antibiotic to the mother and assumed a defensive position with the rest of the platoon. The rifle fire stopped suddenly, and we waited on alert for an enemy encounter.

Within a short period of time, another platoon of Marines showed up with a grizzled staff sergeant who spotted me immediately. He asked if I'd like an escort back to the compound. I was so relieved I wanted to hug him but realized that would get me a slap in the face. I enthusiastically accepted his escort offer. The other Marines in the platoon were quite comfortable with merging their numbers with the new platoon.

I later learned from the arriving platoon that the gunfire was from friendly South Vietnamese troops that had arrived back home near the village. They were told to test fire their weapons to guarantee they were empty. Those soldiers were so untrained that inevitably there were rounds left in the chamber. The rounds were fired into the air when the troops cleared their weapons. Much to my relief, we arrived back at the Marine compound in short order without further incident.

For a brief moment, I'd experienced the dread and intense fear of waiting for incoming fire. It helped me understand the fear and reaction of the psychological casualties I worked with through-out the year. The fact that my encounter was relatively short-lived and benign did not relieve me of the stress of living in a war zone. We did get hit at the wire shortly after I arrived, and I fell out of my hut with my .45 and went to the wire line to support the Marine defenders. Although I fired my weapon, I'm not sure I ever hit anything, and it was a pitiful attempt to contribute to the organized firepower of the Marine troops.

The next morning, I found a gunny sergeant and discussed my concern that my .45 seemed to be totally inadequate as a de-fense weapon. He agreed with a commanding, "Yes, Sir!" I asked if he could help, and he again said his robust, "Yes, Sir!" He said he'd be back later that afternoon. When he arrived, he had a weapon I didn't recognize, but it turned out to be a Thompson submachine gun. The weapon fired the same rounds used in my .45, but it was an automatic weapon, and in competent hands was an excellent defense weapon.

He took me to the range where he'd set up fifty-five-gallon drums about thirty-five to fifty yards away. He showed me how to load the weapon and told me he'd selected that one since it was the only machine gun available that fired the first round with a double action trigger. That meant a round could be chambered, and it would immediately fire with the safety off and a pull of the trigger, then go into automatic mode.

The operation was different from other automatic weapons where you usually had to chamber a round to get the first round to fire. He told me to shoot the fifty-five-gallon drum, but as I pulled the trigger, the weapon climbed so quickly, I was soon shooting directly overhead. He got a laugh out of that and taught me to start out firing pointing low. I soon learned that as the weapon climbed, I could hit the drums.

I must say that the staff sergeants and gunny sergeants became my idols. They took care of me but still respected me, and I treated them with the respect and appropriate deference they deserved. They seemed to appreciate a medical officer who valued their training, input, courage, and ability to do their duty in combat. I admired those men and saw very few as psychological casualties. Most of them were quite experienced and were strong, confident personalities who knew how to take care of their Marines. They'd fight to the death to defend those under their command.

For the next thirteen months, any time I had an issue, I looked up a gunny or staff sergeant and immediately got an answer, support, and cooperation. Along with the excellent Marine officers, they're obviously the "backbone" of the Marine Corps. They made the Marines a highly effective fighting force in the difficult combat situations that defined the war in Vietnam.

The Marines built me a small wooden office next to the ten-bed open-air ward where I could keep troops for a few days if they didn't require immediate evacuation for their War-Damage. I saw about nine hundred psychological combat casualties the thirteen months I was in Vietnam, and I became a much better psychologist, basically learning my profession there.

I probably wouldn't want to do it again, but I have some fond memories of my time in Vietnam. I was able to help young men with significant psychological trauma. With my professional growth came a tendency to evacuate more casualties than early on in my tour. Even if they didn't appear as psychologically shattered as the earlier Marines I evacuated, I became increasingly aware that less obvious War-Damage could cause permanent PTSD that might impact them the rest of their lives.

Those I could house in my ward for a few days and work through their trauma responded well. By immediately talking through their War-Damage, the loss of their buddies, and their emotional distress, they were able to decompress, rebuild self-confidence, and often rejoin their units. The ones I could treat "in-country" recovered quickly as the War-Damage was fresh and easily identified as a legitimate and external event unrelated to their emotional stability, worth, or basic personality. In spite of our front-line efforts, many of those War-Damaged Marines needed evacuation, as they had been traumatized beyond the treatment we could provide. Such Marines were not psychologically equipped to experience further War-Damage without permanent psychological injury.

I evacuated those Marines to hospital ships, Japan, or home in an attempt to spare them lingering PTSD injury. My highly competent commander backed me in those decisions, and I feel we were successful in sparing many of those Marines life-long War-Damage symptoms. I became increasingly confident in my instincts and judgment regarding War-Damage. It was often necessary to process many psychological casualties in a short period of time when a company was experiencing heavy losses. That also made it necessary to evacuate more casualties out of the country rather than treat them in my limited space.

One night in early July 1967 stands out in my mind as Alpha and Bravo Companies 1st Battalion Ninth Marines were basically massacred in operation "Buffalo" near Con Thien. Some of their new M-16 rifles (without a chromed bolt and with defective ammunition) jammed during battle, commonly referred to as "firefights." The 90th NVA Regiment overran the 1st/9th Marines' position and killed 84, wounded 190, and 9 were left missing in action out of a force of 400. The next morning, when we were finally able to get into the area, we found dozens of Marines lying on their sides, having been shot at close range while attempting to clear their jammed (defective) weapons. Only twenty-seven Marines from Bravo and about ninety from Alpha were fit for duty after the first day of battle.

How do we get young men to serve us so bravely? One technique involved visualization and acceptance of death in combat. It seemed to relieve those able to undertake the process, relieving some of the dread and some of the pressure of waiting to be killed. This became the source of the expression Marines used when tasked with a dangerous mission: "Don't mean nothing, Sir." This simple acceptance that they might very well not leave Vietnam alive seemingly helped reduce combat stress for some Marines; therefore, they were able to return home with fewer disruptive PTSD symptoms.

During that horrible night in July of '67 when so many Marines were killed, I was asked to help out the Graves Registration unit. This was the 3rd Marine Division support unit that gathered and prepared dead bodies to return stateside. I don't know how many young Marines I carried off choppers that night and lined up side-by-side in rows so a medical doctor could declare them dead. At one point, I must have had twenty to twenty-five men laid out. Even today I still see sharp images of all those bodies, and I can I still vividly recall trying hard to handle those brave Marines as tenderly and respectfully as possible. It was especially difficult knowing they had been sacrificed so needlessly due to their defective weapons.

That was one of the nights that solidified my conviction that war is futile. Thank God we have such young men and women willing to defend our country, but unless the homeland is directly threatened, the pursuit of war in foreign lands seems to accomplish little. I have to say that the Marines I was associated with were generous and caring young men. If a child asked for a stick of gum, the Marine usually gave the child the entire pack. The Marines and Seabees built roads, bridges, schools, and churches with amazing generosity. Children would line the roads as Marines drove by in military vehicles and happily ask for candy and favors that were generously distributed by the Marines.

The commander came to me shortly after I arrived at the medical compound in Phu Bai and observed that I didn't appear to drink a lot. He therefore put me in charge of our local officer's club, which was essentially a converted shower that worked in reverse and flooded the floor during the monsoon season. That gave me supervision over the local civilian staff who worked the bar but were required to stay onsite behind the defenses of the compound at night since it wasn't safe for them to go home after dark.

I gained a great deal of valuable knowledge from those young ladies who learned to speak reasonable English, and for the most part, were often Catholic refugees from North Vietnam. They'd left North Vietnam as Ho Chi Minh pressured the Catholics, but nevertheless, they still had more respect for Ho Chi Minh than they had for the leaders in South Vietnam whom they saw as corrupt and power hungry.

I also had occasion to interview enemy captives who were sent to me after the Marines had finished interrogating them. The Marine Corps wanted additional intelligence regarding the captive's background, training and home location. I could usually get those young men to talk through our interpreter, and I found many of them disgusted with war and hardened to the fact that there was "no win" in the war for them. Some of those troops had families who had been through numerous conflicts all the way back to the French in the 1930s and 1950s, and they just wanted to be left alone. They didn't particularly value communism, and they often hated Red China and the conquering aspirations of the Chinese.

At the risk of alienating politicians associated with the Vietnam War, I want to say that while I have tremendous respect and appreciation for the combat troops of the United States, it was revealing to get to know the Vietnamese people. My direct contact with the people of both South and North Vietnam and prisoners of war allowed me to come to the very firm conclusion that we made a tremendous mistake with the Vietnam War. We should have left Ho Chi Minh alone, and he would certainly have taken over Cambodia and Laos. Considering the horrible events that occurred in Laos and Cambodia, Ho Chi Minh could have been the best thing for those countries.

We would have had a communist country controlled by Ho Chi Minh that was suspicious of Red China, our real concern at that point. Essentially, we would have had a version of "Marshal Tito" similar to Yugoslavia—communist, yes, but possibly willing to work with the United States government. We could have saved the fifty-eight thousand American troops lost during the Vietnam War, and we would have saved Southeast Asia by not decimating North and South Vietnam.

I found the Vietnamese people delightful. They're a gentle race of people who are dedicated to caring for their families and children. They're respectful and appreciative of things they receive from outsiders. We now find this to be true as we're re-engaging with Vietnam on a social, political, and trade basis. In my respectful opinion, we desperately need to learn those lessons and quit trying to shape the world in our image and impose a democratic process that countries are not ready for and do not aspire to follow. So much for my sermon, but I do feel I was in a unique position to make those observations, and I find myself disappointed that we seem to ignore history and not learn from our own recent experiences.

Chapter 5

COMBAT ZONE WAR-DAMAGE

I sincerely believe that there are few human traumas more psychologically damaging than war and the holocaust against the Jews. I have also come to accept the basic truth that we all have a breaking point when faced with extreme stress. Although I personally survived the horrors of war reasonably well, I still carry a few War-Damage symptoms forty years later. My wife of 35 years knows to never wake me up by touching me. Even decades after my war experience, I tend to come up fighting and angry. Every night the last thing I do is lock every door and window in the house. I learned in war that to be surprised is deadly (I am protecting those inside rather than just trying to keep the bad guys out).

For years I startled easily, and if a car backfired on the street, I sometimes found myself prone on the sidewalk. People looked at me strangely, and I felt a little silly, but I damn sure was not going to get shot. I still carefully evaluate strangers in crowds, and my senses are extremely acute at night. I keep a firearm available at all times, I know how to use it, and I know I will if required. I also have the skills and confidence never to use it unnecessarily. That knowledge and the weapon remain a constant comfort, a carryover over from learning combat survival.

Some of the division's medical doctors were also psychological casualties. The pattern was often the same for those who couldn't tolerate the daily stress of living in a war zone. Without being disrespectful of any particular group or area of the country, I found that if the doctor was raised on a farm in Texas, Alabama, Louisiana, or was from the Midwest, they often did quite well. If they were from the coastlines of California or New York etc., and they'd grown up pampered and rich, they couldn't always take the stress of a combat theater. I'd find them standing on their bunks to put on their clothes, usually a sign they were in trouble. In all fairness, the fact that our medical doctors had to take care of torn up young men with life debilitating injuries day after day was extremely hard on them.

I recall one surgeon who had a significant psychological crisis but was such a strong personality he remained with the unit. A "Bouncing Betty" (an anti-personal mine that bounces in the air before exploding) had hit a former Olympic wrestler. Both arms and legs were crippled, and he was blind and initially deaf. Because he was wearing body protection and was evacuated so quickly, the surgeon was able to save him.

The next day, I saw the surgeon who was in serious psychological distress, questioning what he had done saving such a talented athlete now destined to be a cripple. This fine surgeon had a strong personality and was such a talented doctor that I was able to talk him through his upset and keep him with the unit. Thank God for the talented medical personnel who can tolerate the stress of mending horrific combat injuries and still carry on. The military doctors and corpsmen are more essential to a combat theater than we can ever imagine or properly acknowledge. They're not always adequately recognized or appreciated, but without them and everything they provide, combat troops and their dangerous service could not survive.

It was my assumption before going to Vietnam that combat stresses and War-Damage were primarily the result of combat trauma. This is not necessarily true, although actual combat is certainly one of the primarily causes of PTSD. War-Damage is also the result of prolonged stress in a combat theater even for support area troops.

I learned this stress lesson myself when I found out that I had only six seconds from hearing mortars leave the tube until they hit the compound. To help adjust to my daily worry of mortar attacks, I put a pulley on my mosquito net so I could yank it off in a single second. I re-hung the screen door to my hut so it opened facing my personal bunker. A gunny helped me borrow (*gunny-rescued*) runway steel matting from the Seabees that I layered over the sandbags of my one-person bunker, and I was all set.

I learned to wake up at the sound of mortars firing, pull my mosquito net, and dive through the door and into my bunker in a little less than the six seconds it took the mortars to arrive. That probably gave me a false sense of safety, but I did find a piece of shrapnel in the middle of my bunk one night after one of our infrequent mortar attacks. That confirmed the need for my preparations and reduced my fear of mortar attacks.

One newly arrived doctor insisted on showing his fearless demeanor by sleeping nude each night in the jungle humidity. Most of us suspected he enjoyed the female reaction of the teenage locals who came in early to sweep the floor and gather the laundry. He proudly slept on his back each morning awaiting what he must have thought were admiring young girls. When we arrived at the field hospital, we were all issued helmets and flak jackets that most of us kept under our cots for easy access. The new doc disdained this protection and stored his gear on the wall in an unhandy location.

One night, about 2:00 a.m., the mortars arrived. We all rushed to the group bunker I still used at that point, wearing our helmets and flak jackets. The newbie showed up nude sans helmet and flak jacket and rushed inside the unlighted bunker. In the dark, he sat down on a large gecko lizard. Those common jungle inhabitants didn't normally bite, but they could make an awful screech. The thrashing gecko wiggling under the doc's rear end, close to his pride and joy, caused him to jump up quickly. In the process of suddenly standing, the newbie hit his exposed head on an overhead 4x4 wood support beam. He was out cold for much of the mortar attack. Needless to say, that was his first and last nude bunker foray.

I developed extreme confidence in the fact that our Marines would fight to the death to defend our compound. That reassurance, plus my own preparations, allowed me to tolerate the stresses of a combat zone and function effectively as the division psychologist. Although I didn't experience frequent physical combat, I nevertheless came home with a certain amount of War-Damage from living months in a dangerous support compound. At the end of my thirteen-month tour, I departed Da Nang direct from a combat zone and seventeen hours later arrived at the San Francisco Airport. Nothing but loud music, honking cars, and selfish drivers. Not exactly dangerous or life threatening but my stress and anxiety did not subside.

The transition was too quick. I came home retaining the necessary alert skills and survival reactions, otherwise known as "CSS" (Combat Survival Skills-My term for lingering combat-awareness), necessary to tolerate living in a combat zone. One of these is an instant flash of attack anger. In a combat zone, when the "sauce hits the pan" (notice I cleaned that up a little), you better get angry and ready to fight. Being afraid rather than angry or running away gets you killed. Getting angry fast and fighting keeps you alive. You therefore develop an instinctive and innate anger response, alertness, and fighting spirit that helps you survive.

The day after I arrived back home in Stockton, California, I was driving a car and had stopped at a red light. I didn't move quickly enough when it turned green, and the woman behind me started honking. My anger flashed in an instant. I jumped out of the car quickly and headed back toward her. When I reached the hood of her car, I saw her face. She was scared to death, and I must have looked like the devil himself. As a psychologist, I certainly knew better and shouldn't have had such a reaction, but my CSS survival anger had kicked in. I stopped, turned around, and went back to my car. I was six feet three inches tall and weighed 205 pounds. Certainly, I appeared threatening and dangerous to a 130-pound woman.

The CSS response combat veterans bring home is repressed and unexpected. But, it's *hardwired*, *automatic*, and *instant*. There's no voluntary *off* switch veterans can use to prevent defensive, abrupt, and scary reactions. He/she has developed an internal and automatic lifesaving ability over weeks of time to survive the dangers and debilitating stress found daily in all combat zones. The response is like breathing and seems normal, necessary, and comfortable. Our CSS is part of our uniform, we wear it with pride and confidence, and it will protect us at all times.

When I got home after my CSS behavior at the stoplight, my father found out what had happened. He was a street-smart man who never finished high school but could have been a psychologist himself. He immediately told me to pack my bag because we were going to Canada hunting for three weeks. The long car trip to

Canada and back, plus three weeks in the woods, let me decompress and emotionally relax.

I had grown up hunting most of my childhood while living on the Indian reservation. For the three years we lived there, we had reservation permission to hunt deer for food and the hunting trip seemed an obvious answer to my concerned father. Despite my childhood history, I found that I couldn't kill anything on that trip to Canada. I didn't even shoot at the elk my dad herded right in front of me. I guess I'd seen too much killing during the war because I haven't wanted to hunt or kill anything since.

This pattern of residual anger also showed up when I interacted with members of my family who had long looked forward to my safe return. Flashes of "combat-anger" occurred mostly with my younger sister. She was still a teenager, and as the only girl and baby of the family, was understandably spoiled. She was less than enthused about an older brother intruding on her space and her privileged status. I was curt with her demands, and was unnecessarily critical of her behavior. Instead of welcoming her presence, I rejected her, usually with aggressive behavior of my own. My outbursts often included swearing and threatening comments inappropriate to the situation at hand.

Years later, I discussed my behavior with my sister. Even now she still has clear memories of her confusion with my behavior and remembers being upset with me at the time. The unintended damage we do to important interpersonal relationships because of our return with CSS and War-Damage can last a long time and disrupt relationships for years.

Residual War-Damage remains when veterans are moved too quickly and without adjustment intervention from a combat zone back home. This explains why marriages can get off to such a rough re-start. The long absent veterans are often met by loving wives, husbands, girlfriends, boyfriends, and parents who have no knowledge of the war stress their loved one has been through and brings home. Both the returning veteran and those who have been waiting for them have little awareness or understanding of the hardwired combat skills that were necessary to survive in a combat zone. After a few undeserved rejections and unexplained outbursts of anger in the face of attempts to make a caring connection, the damage may become permanent.

Fortunately, there are two beings on earth capable of miti-gating the damage done by the veterans and the relationships they may have destroyed—caring, gentle women and specially trained dogs. .Forgive me the comparison, but both of these "special be-ings" provide the unselfish attention, acceptance, and reassurance the War-Damaged veteran needs. I've labeled this automatic, car-ing, intuitive awareness UPR (Unconditional Positive Regard).

This is the same reassuring response grandparents often pro-vide to children. A grandchild drops their ice cream cone on the sidewalk, and the grandparent buys another—"UPR." The parent might complain that they're spoiling the child. In actuality, the child feels better, understands their still valued despite the mistake, and has increased self-confidence regarding his/her relationship with the grandparents. This is exactly what War-Damaged veter-ans need from a source providing UPR.

My father's Canadian trip and the associated decompression let me partially blunt my War-Damage and the residual symptoms of PTSD. The unknown CSS was still there, however, and quickly showed up when I reported for duty as the staff psychologist at the naval hospital in Jacksonville, Florida. One morning, I was walking in my service whites from the car to the hospital with three nurses. Being lonely for female "round-eyed" attention, I was flirting with the new nurses when suddenly the naval base fired off automatic weapons associated with an aircraft they were repairing.

I immediately hit the tarmac in my service whites, and my round white officer's cover rolled down the parking lot in front of the nurses. I was appropriately embarrassed, and the nurses were immediately concerned. They rushed over with worried looks and knelt down, asking if I was all right. My sheepish smile gave away my embarrassment. I reassured them it was an automatic combat reaction, but I was surely safe from the gunfire in my prone position. We all laughed, and it was the one time my CSS response actually helped. I was able to get dinner dates for the next two weekends.

It took several years to get over my residual anger and resolve my tendency to be unnecessarily critical, harsh, or impatient with loved ones. As a divorced officer, I had nurses available at the hospital who were pleased to give me their attention. I ran most of them off, probably because I was afraid of getting close to anybody, especially a young lady, because things might not work out, or because I was still afraid I might get killed on any given day.

I finally found a woman who had lost her Navy pilot husband in the disaster on the flight deck of the aircraft carrier USS *Forrestal*. She understood me better, was more forgiving, and tolerated my criticism, correction, and outbursts of anger. We were together for years and came close to marriage. Ultimately, it became obvious that her forgiving, southern ways and my hard-charging, task-oriented personality were probably not compatible. We parted friends, but I have forever felt that lingering War-Damage contaminated an opportunity to marry a life-long companion.

To illustrate that War-Damage leads to post-traumatic

stress, a couple of typical examples are worth sharing. The first that comes to mind—an enlisted psychological casualty evacuated from an ambush who arrived in dirty combat fatigues immediately off a rescue helicopter. He'd been evacuated by cable withdrawal through the jungle after working hours to save his wounded lieutenant. The lieutenant had taken a round through the chest that prevented him from breathing. In association with his buddies, the Marine continued mouth-to-mouth resuscitation and kept the lieutenant alive many minutes.

Finally, a helicopter arrived, and they attached the lieutenant to a basket with a buddy to help him breathe and raised them through the jungle canopy. About the time they got to the helicopter, the Vietcong hit the helicopter with a rocket propelled grenade (RPG). The helicopter crashed, killing everyone onboard, including the lieutenant and the Marine's basket-riding friend.

The Marine understandably came apart and was evacuated from the field as a psychological casualty. When I saw him, he was still shaking, crying and emotionally devastated. I was taking in so many casualties, I didn't have time to treat him, so I immediately evacuated him to a hospital in Japan. I've always hoped that he made it and have always lamented that there were not a few days to spend with him. I may have been able to help him work through his trauma, and perhaps I could have helped him have a better chance at a normal life.

Another incident that still stands out in my mind concerned an experienced Marine staff sergeant who was leading a four-man reconnaissance patrol behind enemy lines to watch activity on the Ho Chi Minh Trail. He was a well-trained Marine in charge of an elite recon squad. He navigated strange terrain at night and could repair radios, broken legs, firearms, etc. He was trained in camouflage, setting up defensive positions, and "SERE" (Survival, Evasion, Resistance, and Escape). After four days of trail observation, his unit was detected. They had to bug out quickly, and in the process of a forced evacuation, they had to cross a swollen river. His radioman was running last while carrying the heavy radio. Unknown to the rest of the squad, the radioman slipped on the wet rocks and got lodged between two boulders in the middle of the river.

The other three Marines escaped to the far bank, but by the time they took cover and turned around, the enemy had shown up. The three Marines established covering fire, but the enemy kept shooting the radioman lodged in a partially upright position between the boulders. They seemed careful not to kill him at first, shooting him in the arms and legs. The wounds caused repeated screams of agony from the radioman.

The three remaining Marines sought to rescue him but were immediately under heavy fire from an overwhelming force. They had to sit behind cover and defend their radioman as best they could for a prolonged period of time while the enemy continued to shoot him and the radio. Ultimately, the man died, and the squad was able to escape, but they couldn't recover their comrade. I saw the staff sergeant shortly after his return, and he was a haunted man. He was a strong, talented Marine, but the stress of losing his radioman and having to watch the prolonged agony of his death really impacted him.

I had time to work with him over several days, and as you would expect from such a strong person, he came around quickly. I was reluctant to send him back to his combat unit, but he insisted that he was ready, and it was what he wanted to do. His unit obviously needed him and also pressured me for his return.

I reluctantly agreed to his request, and I'm reasonably confident he did well. It is nevertheless not surprising that even that strong, experienced, and courageous man proved to have a breaking point, as do we all under sufficient stress.

In a combat zone, you don't have to be shot at to break under pressure. The prolonged threat of injury or death by adversaries who want to kill you is all it takes. War-Damage is further compounded by the corrosive guilt Marines experience if they haven't been able to continue with their unit or if they break down from the prolonged stress of a rear area. There's nothing serene or relaxing about living in a combat zone.

Please hold your skepticism about veterans with War-Damage who only served in the support area in a combat zone. They have earned their CSS and residual symptoms legitimately. The fact that they have carried their emotional stress to civilian life is understandable and needs attention. Their tendency to drink excessively, use drugs, and be difficult with their wives or loved ones is predictable. These young women and men need our support and understanding, despite how unpleasant their behavior and destructive it become.

My combat experience with our brave and worthy Marines made me into a dedicated patriot. I know of no other army in the world as caring and constructive as the U.S. military. I am proud of my service, despite my criticism of the Vietnam war's outcome. I'm finally comfortable wearing my Vietnam hat and windbreaker in public after years of silence about my service.

Chapter 6
WHY IT DIDN'T WORK IN VIETNAM

Marines returned from Vietnam two different ways. Some rotated as intact companies or battalions with their commanding officers in place. Many of those Marines came on slow moving ships with military equipment, weapons, and hardware being returned to the United States. The ships took days of time to reach Hawaii, during which knowledgeable commanders didn't allow the ship's company to use the Marines for shipboard tasks, such as swabbing the decks, cleaning the latrines, or handling KP duties.

That allowed the Marines time to relax, talk, read, goof-off, and enjoy the ship's sunny decks. Many of those Marines essentially participated in non-formal, but helpful, "Exposure Therapy." By spontaneously sharing their combat experiences with other veterans, some were able to slowly lessen the anxiety, anger, and aggression associated with active combat. That process of slowly returning Marines to the "world" served the purpose of getting the veterans home, while also allowing for an important period of decompression and modest insight about how they might have changed during combat. They were proud and respectful of completing their mission, and on some occasions, they returned the "Colors of the Regiment" to their home base.

Another way home involved Marines rotating individually or in small groups. They were transported by commercial jets from a combat zone "back to the world" in a seventeen-plus-hour flight. Although enthused to be out of the combat zone, those Marines were often disappointed in what they first experienced stateside.

I experienced that phenomenon myself when I flew for seventeen hours from Da Nang to California in a plane full of Marines. We were dressed in various clothing, from combat fatigues to civilian clothing normally used during "Rest and Relaxation" (R&R) trips. I landed unexpectedly at the San Francisco airport to refuel ahead of the short flight to the military base where we were originally scheduled to land.

Upon deplaning for refueling, we were herded through an area filled with civilians waiting to catch their planes. A group of civilians immediately recognized we were returning combat Marines and started to chant disrespectful slogans such as "baby killers" and other terms like "jungle bunnies," etc. Some of them even went so far as to throw food or water bottles at us while yelling "grenade," or "in-coming." The anger and hatred in those comments weren't lost on me and were immediately depressing. I came back proud of my service and naïvely expected appreciation for the sacrifices and trauma of thirteen months in a dangerous foreign war. Instead, I found disrespect, ridicule, and accusation.

This reception had a jarring impact on my comfort and confidence returning to the "world." Instead of being proud and accepted, I felt misunderstood, dismissed, and rejected. The ridicule and rejection from my homeland forced me to hide my status as a combat veteran. The lingering effect of that initial trauma and the prevalent ridicule caused me to be silent for years about my military service and especially my combat duty. It was as though I was hiding some secret sin, I'd committed, though I certainly had no sense of having done wrong. I felt like a pariah among my fellow

Americans. I even found myself hiding my recent duty from fellow Navy personnel at the hospital in Jacksonville where I served as staff psychologist for a year.

I couldn't express pride in my combat role for my country or share my constructive contribution during my military service. The extent of my service repression came home at age seventy-six when I had to furnish my DD-214 discharge papers while obtaining a concealed firearm license. I was completely shocked to see I'd received two Bronze Stars for my service in Vietnam. That star is a military decoration awarded for heroic or meritorious service in a combat zone. I'm not sure of the specifics related to those medals, but my emotional distance from my combat service had repressed that awareness for over forty-five years.

The lack of respect, acceptance, and recognition of those traumatic years in Vietnam caused me to ignore and repress much of my lingering War-Damage. The concern about being misunderstood or disliked only furthered my marginal adjustment after returning from a combat zone. Count my experience as typical of hundreds of thousands of troops returning from Vietnam or current wars in the Middle East.

The initial civilian reactions, plus our limited understanding of the need to deal with the stresses of combat in a timely way, led to the prolonged agony that many of our Vietnam veterans experienced when they arrived home. They were neither offered nor given any approval or acceptance for their sacrifice and no help to deal with their unresolved War-Damage. Fellow citizens didn't appreciate their hazardous duty and combat service. For years we ignored most of those troops, with the horrible results of homelessness, suicides, and broken marriages, which have been well documented for the past several decades.

Are we making the same mistake again with our brave combat veterans from the Middle East? Most of them are better trained, have better skills, and are led by officers who have a better understanding and appreciation for the trauma of combat stress. However, the fact that we're sending them back for multiple tours probably overrides the constructive aspects of better training and officers who are more aware. We may again be building a thirty-to-fifty- year legacy of damaged men and women with distressed lives who will need individual care for years. What they really need is effective attention on their way home before they try to resume a normal life, in order to resolve the psychological stresses of living and performing in a combat zone .

The combat stress and War-Damage of Vietnam is not a new phenomenon. In previous wars, combat stress was known as "shell shock" and "combat fatigue." Essentially, the stresses were the same, and the destructive symptoms of agitation, anxiety, depression, and anger were similar. Vietnam Marines also experienced continual action in a fierce combat environment with minimal sleep, monsoon rains, significant summer heat, high humidity that drained energy, poor hygiene, and a myriad of jungle diseases. All those daily external factors were always present and uncontrollable. Those issues had an added effect to the corrosive combat stresses for the grunts in the bush.

Major differences in the Vietnam War were the intensity and duration of the actual combat experience. In World War II, in the South Pacific, the average Marine spent approximately forty days in combat. In Vietnam, the average infantryman spent 240 days during a year in a combat environment.[3] That was due to helicopters' abilities to move them quickly in and out of the field and respond immediately to changing combat needs.

In some ways, the troops were a little different. During World War II the average age was nineteen or twenty, whereas the average age in Vietnam was twenty-three. Seventy-five percent of the combat vets in Vietnam were high school educated, and many were drafted, although two thirds were volunteers. In fact, 70 percent of those killed in action in Vietnam were volunteers. Many may have volunteered to avoid the draft they were likely to experience due to a low draft number. Many signed up for combat duty prior to being drafted. Ninety-seven percent of them were honorably discharged, and most completed their full tour of military duty.

There were 58,210 troops killed in Vietnam. Approximately 304,000 were wounded and 75,000 were severely disabled, which was approximately *300 percent* higher than comparable numbers in World War II. The Vietnam Helicopter Pilots Association last updated those statistics on January 1, 2011.[1] From the Department of Veteran Affairs,[4] we now know there are approximately 400,000 homeless Veterans in this country, of which 47 percent served in Vietnam. Of the Vietnam veterans, 67 percent served their country for at least three years, and 33 percent were stationed in a war zone. Veterans account for approximately 23 percent of all the homeless people in America.

The Veteran's Affairs Office notes,[2] "A large number of displaced and at-risk veterans live with lingering effects of PTSD." A further damning statistic notes that the Veterans Administration may reach less than 25 percent of these homeless veterans in need, leaving around three hundred thousand literally "out in the cold." While those numbers are impossible to confirm, many expert researchers feel these may well be conservative figures.

With the clarity of 20/20 hindsight, let's learn from history and spend the time, money, and energy where it will have the most beneficial impact—namely on the men and women returning from combat when they are most available for successful intervention. At that point, they still have the youth and willpower to overcome the trauma of war and establish productive and independent lives. If we continue to fail our brave combat veterans, history will teach us another cruel lesson and we'll have failed another generation of brave men and women who didn't sign up for lingering PTSD issues as part of their service commitment.

Another critical lesson from history teaches us what works when treating traumatized combat veterans. The Department of Veteran Affairs observes, that effective treatment programs for homeless and at-risk veterans can be community-based non-profit groups. I can personally confirm that this approach works.

The reality is that combat troops don't respond well to naïve civilian "shrinks" or well-intended psychological programs run by college-educated counselors with essentially no combat experience. The troops are often reluctant to engage with these professionals, since once diagnosed and documented to have a mental disorder, the soldier may lose their security clearance, ability to advance within the military, or even work many civilian positions. Well-intended young counselors fresh out of M.D. or Ph.D. programs may well have trouble setting aside their biases against war and combat soldiers. That negative bias is quickly perceived by veterans who see such reactions as typical of the reserved reception they may have received when returning from Vietnam. Thankfully, the better reception our current veterans experience is reassuring and constructive.

In recent years, the VA has recognized the destructive nature of exposure to Agent Orange. Many of the related health problems didn't show up for years and were so subtle, the medical community didn't make the connection to Vietnam and Agent

Orange. Veterans are now receiving deserved disability benefits for long-term medical issues recognized to be related to Agent Orange exposure.

A positive note at the Veterans Administration relates to the numerous compliments directed at the available doctors and staff once veterans get past the frequent administrative hurdles and scheduling delays. Evidently, the VA has many good doctors and talented staff, and we need to make them more available in a timely way. Hopefully, the growing negative feedback the Veterans Administration has received will prompt immediate changes that will make this valuable government program more efficient and available.

The troops returning today from the Middle East are much better received, appreciated, and recognized. This is extremely beneficial in helping to dissipate combat stress and the destructive history of serving in a combat zone. I was amazed and pleasantly reassured while waiting for an airplane in Bangor, Maine. A group of troops returning from the Middle East disembarked their aircraft. Immediately, the civilian crowd stood in two lines on each side of the disembarking troops cheering, clapping, and shaking hands with the young men and women as they entered the terminal area.

I joined the crowd and found it rewarding shaking hands with the female and male veterans. It was good to see them smile and appreciate the welcome they were receiving. That simple act of kindness and appreciation by the civilians in the Bangor airport was evidently a common phenomenon. Many planes land there to refuel before traveling south and west to the rest of the United States. That reception has become traditional for the citizens of Maine, and they deserve a lot of credit for their kind consideration and appreciation of our troops returning from combat.

Chapter 7

CAUSES OF WAR-DAMAGE

War is destructive to human beings. This is true of both men and women in a combat zone. To survive, certain internal adjustments must be made. They include being on constant alert, being sensitive to certain sounds, and being suspicious of unknowns including people and places. Combat troops develop a heightened awareness of security issues and the instant availability of adrenaline for a fight or flight response.

These internal adjustments to our mental status and physical surroundings are crucial in a combat zone. The more direct and repeated the experience with actual combat, the more intense are the necessary adjustments. Female troops have the additional constant threat of possible abuse due to their close proximity to hundreds of female-deprived male troops, as well as the additional stress of being captured and abused by the enemy. The assault dangers affecting our female troops in a combat zone certainly approach the level of stress and trauma experienced by troops during horrific combat encounters. This issue is well stated in Jama Psychiatry 1915 with the title of, *Prevalence of Posttraumatic Stress Disorder in Vietnam-Era Women Veterans.* Vietnam service significantly increased the odds of PTSD relative to US service; this effect appears to be associated with wartime exposures, especially sexual discrimination or harassment and job performance pressures. Results suggest long-lasting mental health effects of Vietnam-era service among women veterans."[10]

The symptoms of PTSD while in a combat zone are often the same as those upon returning home. The crucial difference is that in a combat zone, many of those reactions are accepted because they're necessary combat survival skills (CSS) and experienced by most of the troops. In a combat zone, those survival adjustments help us tolerate the horrors of war, as well as the constant tension and alertness necessary in a rear-area.

The National Center for PTSD estimates that 31 percent of returning Vietnam male veterans and 27 percent of returning Vietnam female veterans have had PTSD in their lifetimes.[5] That may explain the high homeless population, frequent mental health problems, and high suicide rates among Vietnam veterans.

A flash of anger, cursing, and/or fighting that interrupts a friendship or social relationship is reasonably well tolerated in a combat zone. Lashing out at someone your own size, capable of either physical or mental retaliation, is therefore self-limiting. Combat zone outbursts cause less guilt and regret than doing the same thing to your wife, children, or loved ones when you get home. It's one thing to push, kick, or hit a 180-pound fellow soldier. It's quite another thing to hit a 130-pound wife. The soldier you hit or curse at is not necessarily afraid of you. A single blow to a loving wife, who feels herself devalued and afraid, understandably scares the woman and their children, and may do serious and/or permanent damage to the marriage.

My own experiences with flashes of anger, high startle reaction, constant vigilance inside and outside the home, and critical/destructive comments to siblings and loved ones, was a surprise to me, and initially uncontrolled. I was ready for combat at all times, and the survival skills I'd developed in a combat zone were spontaneous and unreasoning. Those skills didn't serve me well with strangers, friends, and family. I didn't realize I was "War-Damaged," and therefore not the same person who had left home thirteen months earlier. I was back home too soon from the war zone, and I needed time to decompress and adjust to civilian life. The three weeks I spent in Canada with my father helped mitigate many of those sudden and unwarranted angry responses. I returned from that trip more relaxed and partially re-adjusted to rejoining the "world."

The symptoms of PTSD have been well documented by both the VA and professional researchers. This brief summary of symptoms covers the basics for purposes of understanding the solution to helping returning war veterans. An excellent article on symptoms comes from the National Center for PTSD, published in November 2005. It's called "A Guide for Military Personnel,"[6] and it does an excellent job documenting the symptoms and difficulties associated with returning combat troops. The same organization also produced an excellent guide in 2006, titled "A Guild for Families of Military Members (Home Coming)."[6] This guide gives spouses and families an understanding of "combat stress reactions" and the potential effect on family lives. I would encourage spouses, family members, and veterans to look up these two brief articles and the associated research that can be found at the National Center for PTSD website: https://www.ptsd.va.gov/.[5]

Understanding the issues and educating yourself about symptoms and what to expect from returning combat veterans, whether male or female, can be an effective start to tolerating lingering War-Damage issues.

The nature of PTSD reactions falls roughly into three categories:

- Acute – Symptoms occurring immediately or a few months after combat trauma.

- Chronic – Symptoms that last more than three to six months.

- Delayed – At least six months have passed between the trauma and the onset of symptoms.

The intensity of combat trauma often leads to the acute form of PTSD. It's much easier to treat if resolved in a timely way in the combat zone or while returning from the combat zone. Chronic PTSD is likely to show up once the veteran is stateside and cannot adjust to either a civilian or military lifestyle.

Both of those conditions are better treated sooner rather than later and are not well understood or easily resolved by non-veteran professionals who haven't experienced the trauma of war. Yes, I know the old saying, "You do not have to have had a brain tumor to be a brain surgeon." It is the case, however, that former combat troops have credibility and connecting experiences with returning troops that one can never gain through scholastic study or civilian experience. These valuable combat veterans can be found throughout our nation, and we need to find and use them to help resolve our veterans' "War-Damage Cancer" caused by war.

Acute and chronic PTSD often manifest in combat veterans who had stable, pre-war personalities and have been active and productive members of their military units. During their combat in Vietnam or the Middle East, they experienced significant

War-Damage as evidenced by one or more of the following symptoms:

1. They have witnessed or experienced a life-threatening combat event.

2. They have experienced intense feelings of fear, horror, or helplessness while serving in a combat zone.

3. They cannot get the combat details out of their minds, and they experience continuing dreams, flashbacks, and psychological stress when reminded of the event.

4. They have trouble sleeping, concentrating, or staying on task as a result of intrusive memories of combat trauma.

5. They have a high startle reaction, increased irritability, and unexplained outbursts of temper or anger.

6. Their symptoms have persisted more than a month.

7. Their distress is impacting their work, military effectiveness, comfortable interactions with family and friends, and normal day-to-day functioning.

8. These military soldiers are often easy to spot while still in the combat zone. Their immediate leaders know which soldiers are having difficulties. Their inability to function may be resolved by moving them to a more secure rear area or assigning them safer duties in order to allow them to stay in-country. That often requires them to be transferred from their original unit. The assumption is that a less threatening location or job will help relieve

the PTSD symptoms. This approach is often helpful for some combatants and may prevent debilitating guilt or loss of self-confidence.

- If the symptoms still persist while in service, they may have less impact on the military unit since the disturbed solder is in a less demanding social role. Officers and NCOs assume "time will heal" and may therefore make little effort to effect immediate treatment of this "subclinical" War-Damage. Once a soldier returns stateside, the symptoms may persist and interfere with a successful adjustment to civilian life, non-combat military environment or new job. *The ideal treatment window for our returning veterans from direct combat or living in a combat zone is during the process of returning home.*

- PTSD symptoms observed either in combat or once a veteran returns home are usually common to both settings. A limited and hardly exhaustive list of common symptoms include.

1. Alcohol/drug abuse

2. Difficulty falling asleep

3. Nightmares

4. Constant irritability

5. Flashbacks about war events

6. Problems dealing with authority

7. Easily angered to the extreme

8. Difficulty controlling anger

9. Difficulty with superiors, either in the military or at work

10. Anger at society or people in general

11. Hostility/violence

12. Constant tension or anxiety

13. Cannot feel close to family

14. Jumping at slight noises

15. Unable to relax

16. Marital problems

17. Sexual problems

18. Suicidal thoughts

Any of those symptoms may be further rated according to the following:

1. A small problem that has not been a difficulty

2. A moderate problem that has had some minor impact on the veteran's life

3. A serious problem that has made things very difficult for the veteran at unexpected times

4. A critical problem that has caused a major difficulty adjusting to civilian life

The Walter Reed Army Institute of Research (WRAIR)[8] has done excellent research at the Walter Reed Army Hospital as part of the U.S. Army Medical Research and Material Command Division.[9] This research has identified combat issues that may be carried home and gives advance notice of pending PTSD issues. The WRAIR has put together several relevant subcategories to describe residual reactions of the returning veterans. The term they use is *"Residual Mindset"* to identify the auto-response veterans bring home from war.[8]

1. **In a combat zone the "Residual Mindset" is:** You may talk about the mission only with those who need to know, and you only talk about combat experiences with buddies.

   Self-Test Back Home You may avoid sharing any of your deployment experiences with your family, spouse, and friends. You have not shared your deployment experiences with those closest to you and back off or get angry when someone asks about combat experience.

2. **In a Combat zone the "Residual Mindset" is:** Your responsibilities are to achieve the mission and do your best to keep your buddies alive. You may feel you failed your buddies if they were killed or seriously injured. You may be bothered by memories of those wounded or left behind.

   Self-Test Back Home: Combat memories of the deployment keep bothering you. You are still feeling guilty about things that happened in combat.

3. **In a Combat zone the "Residual Mindset" is:** Driving unpredictably fast, using rapid lane changes, and straddling the middle line to keep other vehicles at a

distance is designed to avoid IEDs (improvised explosive devices) and VIEDs (vehicle improvised explosive devices).

Self-Test Back Home: Aggressive driving leads to speeding tickets, accidents, fatalities and chasing adrenaline highs by driving fast while easily angered.

4. **In a Combat** zone **the "Residual Mindset" is:** Survival depends on discipline and obeying orders.

   Self-Test Back Home: Relationships are not going well and ongoing conflicts over decisions and inflexible interactions (ordering and demanding behavior) with your spouse, children, and friends often leads to conflict.

5. **In a Combat zone the "Residual Mindset" is:** Alcohol use is limited, and the penalties for abuse are high.

   Self-Test Back Home: Alcohol is now plentiful and using alcohol to calm down or help you sleep becomes common. Others telling you that you are drinking too much.

6. **In a Combat zone the "Residual Mindset" is:** Survival depends on being aware of your surroundings at all times and reacting immediately to sudden change.

   Self-Test Back Home: Still staying revved up, you may feel keyed up or anxious in large groups or in confined situations, and you are easily startled when you hear loud noises. Frequent nightmares, trouble sleeping and drinking to calm down or help you sleep.

7. **In a Combat zone the "Residual Mindset" is:** Carrying your weapon at all times is mandatory and necessary.

   Self-Test Back Home: You may feel the need to have weapons on you, in your home, or in your car at all times and may threaten someone with a weapon.

8. **In a Combat zone the "Residual Mindset" is:** Controlling your emotions during combat is critical for mission success.

   Self-Test Back Home: Feeling numb. Loved ones tell you that you have really changed. Failing to display emotions or show anger may cause you to be seen as detached and uncaring around family and friends.

9. **Common mistaken assumptions about War-Damage:**

This is my initial training and professional observations working through war-damage with veterans. It is worth keeping these false myths in mind to better understand the difference between PTSD and war-damage.

   Myth 1: Only weak soldiers have mental health problems after surviving in a war zone.

   Fact: Everyone is affected by combat and subsequent war-damage.

   Myth 2: If a soldier has a problem, he/she will get help.

   Fact: Most soldiers do not seek mental help for fear of stigma.

Myth 3: A fellow soldier's mental health problems are none of my business.

Fact: Soldiers most often turn to other soldiers when they need help. Leaders are responsible for helping soldiers but are inadequately trained.

Myth 4: No one can help me if I have a mental health problem.

Fact: Professional treatment helps—the earlier the better.

The public and civilian medical communities tend to lump all combat survival symptoms into a pathological disorder (PTSD). Characterizing legitimate, lifesaving survival skills (necessary in a combat zone) as a mental illness is inappropriate and destructive to the combat veteran.

Below is my attempt to separate residual, combat survival skills from mental health disturbance. It was possible to observe the differences while serving as division psychologist in a war zone and later as staff psychologist at the Jacksonville Naval Hospital. In Jacksonville, I had a year of additional experience with Marines and naval personnel returning with War-Damage symptoms.

I eventually resolved some of *my* combat survival skills (CSS) developed while serving in an intense combat zone. Some of those skills naturally modify to become *civilian* survival skills. In the table below, I've broken down my own experiences with combat reactions and how survival skills can become helpful in civilian life.

COMBAT SURVIVAL SKILLS VERSUS WAR-DAMAGE SYMPTOMS

COMBAT SURVIVOR SKILL	MAY BECOME CIVILIAN SURVIVOR SKILL	POSSIBLE WAR-DAMAGE SYMPTOMS
High startle reaction	Benign civilian survivor skill	
Sensitive to strangers	Benign civilian survivor skill	
Watch your 6 (Behind You)	Benign civilian survivor skill	
Check all doors are locked	Benign civilian survivor skill	
Sensitive to strange noises	Benign civilian survivor skill	
Very light or poor sleeper	Benign civilian survivor skill	
Avoid crowds and public places	Benign civilian survivor skill	
More observer than socializer	Benign civilian survivor skill	
Excessive alcohol abuse		Possible War-Damage symptom
Chronic drug use		Possible War-Damage symptom
Chronic anger reactions		Possible War-Damage symptom
Mental or physical abuse		Possible War-Damage symptom
Inconsistent work ethic		Possible War-Damage symptom
Night terrors/dreams		Possible War-Damage symptom
Difficulty resuming intimacy		Possible War-Damage symptom
Avoiding previous friendships		Possible War-Damage symptom

This is by no means an exhaustive list. They are, rather, examples of obvious behaviors that delineate between potential adaptation from combat to civilian life and disruptive combat carryovers that need professional intervention. Much of this War-Damage carryover can be dealt with by timely discussion with other combat veterans. That's exactly what happens when troops have several weeks to return home on slow ships. They have time to talk and gain understanding and perspective from other veterans who have been through the same thing they've experienced.

Chapter 8

UNDERSTANDING WAR-DAMAGE

Combat stress reactions were very common in World War II where the European troops were exposed to months of combat and the Pacific troops were exposed to extremely intense combat over shorter periods of time. It was usually called either *shell shock* or *combat fatigue.* Most of the troops in WWII were ultimately brought home on slow moving ships with other combat veterans. That allowed them to spend time talking through their combat stress with each other, and it was an excellent example of informal "Exposure Therapy." In discussing their combat experiences with other veterans, they were helping to decompress and dissipate their combat survival skills before returning home. That constructive opportunity was marginally helpful but fell far short of preparing them for quiet civilian life.

There are certainly a percentage of combat veterans who need extensive professional help. Fortunately, most can be helped to adjust and enjoy productive civilian lives with early intervention from timely support programs that recognize combat stress for what it is—a necessary skill to survive in a combat zone that needs to be understood and resolved for a constructive civilian life. The prolonged ship transit home during WWII helped to expose and identify the intense nature of "combat survival skills." After weeks discussing their trauma in combat with buddies, the veterans arrived somewhat better prepared to return to a home setting.

This same exposure and readjustment process, if immediately available on the way home from combat, would serve our veterans well today. With today's rapid flights home, returning veterans have no time or opportunity to adjust from the survival needs of a combat zone to a civilian setting. If War-Damage symptoms are not resolved within six to nine months of coming home, veterans tend to need medication and talk therapies such as cognitive restructuring, stress inoculation training, or exposure therapy to treat what may become chronic PTSD.

- The National Center for PTSD describes **"Cognitive Restructuring"** as an approach in which you identify and examine upsetting thoughts about your trauma, challenge those thoughts, and replace them with more balanced and accurate ones.

- The same organization defines **"Stress Inoculation Training"** as reducing symptoms through anxiety reduction techniques, teaching coping skills, and correcting inaccurate thoughts related to trauma.

- **"Exposure Therapy"** is identified as using careful, detailed imaging of your trauma (exposure) in a safe, controlled environment to help you face and gain control of the fear and distress that was overwhelming during the combat repeated trauma.

- While treating hundreds of psychological casualties in Vietnam, I found these approaches very helpful. The excellent training I received from an Austrian psychiatrist in hypnosis and *"Directed Relaxation Recall"* (my term) of repressed trauma was especially effective. The combination of malnutrition, debilitating fear, fatigue, sudden death of buddies, intense gun fire, explosions, TBI (traumatic brain injury) and sudden relocation from immediate death to a field hospital resurrected seldom seen hysterical conversion reactions such as blindness and physical malfunction. One traumatized Marine arrived totally blind. You could swing a bat at his eyes, and he would not blink or try to dodge the blow. Another Marine could not move the fingers on his shooting hand despite no indication of injury. Both recovered completely after a few sessions of deep relaxation recall.

- All of these treatments usually require intense individual therapy by well-trained professionals. Medications are often used for additional comfort and success during treatment. The regular use of medications is normally part of the training and clinical experience of the professionals. Distressed veterans who are seen by less specialized physicians may be medicated for immediate relief without the "talk therapy" or professional time that helps the medications work.

- This is certainly an understandable approach due to the thousands of veterans coming home every week with War-Damage. The problem is compounded by the limited facilities available through the VA or private physicians. Many combat veterans still fall through the cracks since their symptoms may be less disruptive, not communicated to the appropriate facilities, or because such facilities are not available. The combination of these deficiencies is obviously part of the reason for such a high suicide rate among our present returning veterans.

- Instead of being rushed home from the stress and personal changes required in a combat zone, we need to have returning veterans come to a relaxed "Welcome Home" setting while making the journey back to civilian life. Three weeks of Welcome Home time in a private setting is the magic number. We know from working with debilitating depression that one week is not enough, two weeks may start the recovery, and real progress shows in the third week. Allowing three weeks in a beach setting would give veterans a chance to decompress, gain perspective, and incorporate the civilian adjustment necessary to return home.

- To help facilitate the veteran's understanding of their "hardwired" war-damage and need to dissipate CSS (combat survival skills), we could develop a Combat Veterans Corps (CVC), staffed by active and retired combat veterans. The CVS personnel would serve as facilitators and mentors during the three weeks, and veterans would meet briefly each day in a group of the same eight vets with the same mentor. That would provide opportunities for returning veterans to decompress, acknowledge their changed personalities, and prepare for going home to loved ones and families. This "discussion therapy" (my term) availability for returning combat veterans can be the basis for an inexpensive and effective civilian adjustment while dissipating destructive War-Damage.

Three questions come up regarding establishing a Combat Veterans Corps.

1. How do we find CVC mentors?
2. How do we train them?
3. How would they be paid?

Three reasons why a CVC would work:

1. Combat veterans from all military services would be honored to help other vets and many would be honored to serve.

2. The training is already done with veterans who have been through combat. The returning War-Damaged vets are not crazy, sick, or in need of a professional diagnosis. All they need initially while coming home is someone to get them talking—someone who has been through combat and cares. They *will* talk to a combat veteran. (While visiting K9S For Warriors in Jacksonville, Florida to see vets bonding with their service dogs, I was reminded by the K9 staff of how hard it was to get vets to open up and discuss their combat history. However, as soon as I told the veterans I was a combat vet from Vietnam, they immediately engaged, and we talked easily for over an hour.)

3. To pay CVC facilitators our active duty combat vets can receive service pay as usual with extra for expenses, travel, and time. Retired CVC vets should receive a monthly stipend, plus all expenses for travel, lodging, mentoring, and follow-up support.

The success I had keeping psychological casualties "in-country" for decompression and "discussion therapy" was almost 100 percent. If we were light on daily casualties, I could keep them in my primitive, ten-bed ward for a few days and talk through their emotional War-Damage. If the war theater involved large numbers of Marines in combat, our simple medical facility got overwhelmed. I then had to evacuate most of those Marines off shore to hospital ships or land hospitals since I didn't have facilities to keep them "in-country." I saw some of those Marines later while serving as staff psychologist at the naval hospital in Jacksonville, Florida, or in my private practice after discharge from the Navy. Helping them resolve their symptoms and adjust to a productive civilian life months after they came home took more time and was not as successful as working with the combat veterans I could keep in-country while in Vietnam.

I personally experienced similar adjustment problems upon my own return from the combat zone. The delayed symptoms I experienced adjusting to civilian life were personally corrosive and distressing. Although starved for a female relationship and a loving companion, I often drove women away, despite their attention and interest in a single Navy officer. With those women I was prone to anger, criticism, and was often distant, despite an attractive, available companion. In the one relationship I did develop, I became possessive and paranoid about her legitimate social interactions with friends and other male officers. I slowly came to realize that my problems interacting with young women were related to the combat survival skills I brought home. It took time and a lot of personal insight to understand that I was the problem, not the young women or our relationship.

Eventually, I found myself guarded about any relationship and basically became a "job-focused hermit." I let my task-oriented nature determine my social interactions. My War-Damage ultimately disrupted a planned marriage. I became engaged to a lovely woman who wanted more emotional input and a closer relationship than I could provide. I walked away from the wedding after invitations were sent, much to the trauma and disappointment of my potential bride. Thank goodness I didn't marry my fiancée, as I'm sure I would have messed up the relationship in my "combat maladjusted state."

The disappointment, guilt, and sadness over my decision caused me to revert to an internally protected status. I was thwarted in my desire for a close female companion for about seven years. Due to the emotional War-Damage of thirteen months in a combat zone and coming home too quickly, I had little time or opportunity to understand and deal with the combat survival skills I brought with me. That interpersonal deficit continued for years, despite my civilian practice as a clinical psychologist.

In many ways, my years of "subclinical PTSD" are typical of warriors returning from a combat zone today. I had the guarded, distant, and often disruptive behavior of many returning combat veterans. Having "subclinical combat PTSD" makes returning to a civilian lifestyle with loved ones, family and coworkers confusing and disruptive.

It is my firm conviction from personal experience that "War-Damage" has a corrosive effect on the personality of most veterans. That occurs whether in active combat or in a rear-area combat zone. With the premise that war is a destructive encounter for most veterans, the effort to resolve War-Damage needs to include all troops returning from exposure to a combat zone.

Don't be deceived by the fact that today many troops desire to return for a second, third, or fourth tour. In combat, they have purpose and direction due to the structured nature of the military that gives everyone clear instructions as to what to do and when to do it. They have to perform any task or mission ordered without question. The returning volunteers who sign up for another tour receive acceptance and legitimate recognition from using their combat survival skills for a rewarding purpose. They enjoy the respect, appreciation, and importance of their contribution to the war effort.

In some ways, returning our troops for several tours has added additional War-Damage that may be subclinical but very real when they return home. The result of their being so successful in utilizing their combat skills and war-adjusted personalities in a war zone is that they initially appear happy and free of War-Damage symptoms for a few months when they first return. Unfortunately, many veterans returning from either one or multiple tours in the Middle East come home with PTSD symptoms that cause them a great deal of trouble adjusting to home and their civilian lifestyle. The fact that we have numerous suicides per month with veterans of all wars and a rapidly increasing suicide rate for veterans from our Middle East conflicts (now up to twenty per day) should alert us to the fact that we're not providing adequate War-Damage repair for our current women and men veterans.

Chapter 9

RESOLVING WAR-DAMAGE

Fortunately, America is a generous nation. Many pro-active charities and organizations designed to help returning veterans have been created with great success. I'll mention three that are known to me to be useful and effective. There are certainly many others that are providing care, support, and needed help to our veterans.

One unique organization is known as **Folds of Honor**. They've been helping veteran families obtain the funds necessary to educate their children. Many of those funds come directly from Folds of Honor, as well as other generous Americans who help the organization fund scholarships for veterans' children. The value of that organization cannot be overemphasized. Taking care of the children of veterans is a step toward addressing the destructive symptoms of PTSD. If the veteran returns home with unresolved War-Damage, then he or she may not be a capable parent. That can result in anxious, confused children, and the stress of War-Damage extends, possibly leading to mental health problems for the children. Parents and veterans greatly appreciate the grant money that helps take care of their children's needs, and it's especially helpful for veterans who may have limited earning potential due to combat injury or debilitating stress.

Another organization is **Wounded Warriors**. They focus on both the mental and physical problems of returning veterans.

They're dedicated to supplying funds for extensive and often expensive surgeries, as well as providing prosthetic limbs and the necessary training to our gravely injured veterans. They're also available to help with the psychological and emotional needs of veterans. They provide support to spouses and families as the long physical and/or mental recuperation continues. In a twist of irony, those severe injuries may help dissipate the "hard-wiring" of combat survival. The fact of being needy, and the reassurance of caring help over time, may allow the decompression and new perspective combat veterans need to accept and conform to civilian life.

The stress on the caregivers working with Wounded Warriors is tremendous. They spend months to years in daily contact with broken, discouraged veterans who need reassurance, care, and a hand to hold. The fact that these caregivers can vacation at luxurious retreats for leisure and caregiver recovery is both understandable and correct. Wounded Warriors has received some negative publicity about the money spent on such retreats for both program administrators and caregivers. There's little evidence they abuse the dollars associated with those retreats, and what they provide to the caregivers is an excellent investment. Those times to recharge probably help maintain and recruit caregivers, and such retreats undoubtedly contribute to their success with severely injured veterans.

K9s for Warriors fills a unique role helping War-Damaged veterans with chronic PTSD. Such veterans arrive at their doorstep after years of excessive medications and PTSD symptoms. Many have lost numerous jobs, destroyed marital relationships, escaped to excessive drinking or a hermit lifestyle that disrupts social interactions. Their lingering PTSD often keeps them restricted to home and reluctant to interact outside that environment.

They may be reluctant to go shopping in public or even stop by an ATM machine where strangers might appear. What are minor inconveniences to most people become major obstacles for those War-Damaged veterans and their families trying to live a normal lifestyle.

At K9s For Warriors, the veterans are paired with specially trained dogs (usually rescued animals) that are trained by the organization's staff to attend to the needs and anxieties of veterans with PTSD. The dogs are carefully screened for personalities that are not overly aggressive or unpredictable in public and then trained to bond with a War-Damaged veteran. The veterans are housed onsite at "Camp K9." K9s originally used a single house in Ponte Vedra Beach, Florida. Their new facility has now been expanded to a modern campus in St. John's County near Jacksonville, Florida. They can house more veterans at a time, and they work with them to help resolve their PTSD symptoms and bond with their service dogs.

A woman named Shari Duval took no compensation for her initial work starting this fine non-profit. She's known around the campus strictly as "Mom." Shari is a loving, caring individual of high intelligence and good insight into the needs of combat veterans. She treats them with respect, caring, understanding, and provides a valuable asset in the form of the service dogs trained to bond with PTSD stressed veterans. She may help to train other "moms" who serve the veterans. Male and female vets typically live on campus for three weeks. They enjoy good accommodations, meals, and a pleasant, safe atmosphere while they bond with their service dogs.

This generous woman was the heart and soul of the organization's start and initial success. Fortunately, she was blessed to have her talented son, Brett, who came with extensive experience training bomb dogs while an independent consultant with the Department of Defense. Brett served two tours in Iraq and is now an executive of K9s For Warriors.

This organization's work with chronic PTSD cannot be praised enough. The list of veterans who would like to come for training and bond with a service dog grows longer each day. They can now serve more veterans per month in their new facility and are slowly expanding to new locations.

The veterans cherish the love and caring concern they receive from the house "moms" and greatly value the service dogs that so are responsive to the personal attention and care they receive from the veteran. The dogs are initially trained, fed, watered and exercised by a crew of attentive volunteers. They provide the socialization and loving care the dogs need, though they may not necessarily bond specifically with each individual dog.

The dogs are truly amazing. The veterans spend hours of outdoor and social interaction time with their dogs. They walk the dogs in supermarkets, busy restaurants, public parks, etc. This allows the dogs to demonstrate their abilities to understand commands and respond to the combat veteran. It's not unusual in local neighborhoods to walk into a restaurant and see three or four combat veterans with their service dogs quietly residing beneath the table. Civilian guests are often intrigued by the dogs and seldom complain about having animals in the restaurant. Guests are not encouraged to pet or play with the dogs because bonding with the veteran is crucial to the final success of the veteran's relationship with his or her dog.

The dogs are so smart that a veteran can go to an outdoor ATM at the bank and the dog knows to watch his back. The dog is aware of the 180 degrees behind the veteran and is alert to strangers or unusual circumstances that might need the veteran's attention. The veteran is greatly calmed by having the dog on alert and is therefore able to relax and conduct his bank business.

The veterans move throughout the community with their dogs, and the dogs are trained to check around corners or monitor through their keen hearing, sense of smell, and innate instincts anything that might cause the veteran upset or distress. The dogs usually sleep in the same room with the veteran. If the veteran experiences a nightmare or nocturnal flashback, the dog may very well come up and put his head on the veteran's chest to wake him or her. That lets the veteran know that all is calm, and the dog is there to care for and alert them. A few strokes petting the dog, or letting the dog lick their face, and the veteran is able to return to sleep without the upset, sleep disturbance, and trauma of nightmare events.

The veterans and their service dogs return home after three weeks of bonding and training, and the dog becomes a key part of the family. The dogs are the crucial assets needed to return veterans to an active civilian lifestyle. The veterans are finally free of underlying symptoms and the controlling combat survival skills that are contributing to their chronic PTSD. Gentle, caring spouses may provide similar relief from chronic PTSD and are probably more comfortable bed partners. Thus, my earlier comments about the two beings available to help War-Damaged veterans (gentle women and trained dogs).

I can vouch for the fact that the veterans are well treated, well trained, and well served by the K9s For Warriors staff and the service dogs they bond with. We desperately need more such organizations, and they are certainly less expensive than the thirty to fifty years of care some veterans may need through medications and individual appointments with both private and VA doctors.

Chapter 10

THE TIME AND PLACE FOR HELPING COMBAT VETS

The one limitation of the extraordinary programs that serve vets and succeeded over the years, is that they're limited as to how many veterans they can serve. To help the dozens now returning home with War-Damage from the middle east, the real secret is to deal with them as they come home. That timely approach allows for adjustment between being in combat and their returning to civilian lives. There's compelling evidence to show that it would be much cheaper in the long run for us to address the bulk of those veterans on their way home, rather than waiting for destructive PTSD symptoms to interfere with a rewarding civilian life. Fortunately, such a "Welcome Home" program would work equally well for women and men and is just as important to both.

We need to focus on and develop an effective plan to take better care of our returning combat veterans. This pressing need is clearly highlighted by the twenty-plus suicides per day currently experienced by combat veterans returning from duty in the Middle East. We should spend the money and time to help these combat veterans *as they return home*. Timely intervention could dramatically cut down on the disruptive effects of the combat survival skills needed to survive in combat but still retained when they return home.

Those combat skills are hardwired in our veterans and include a high startle reaction, defensive behavior, unpredictable flashes of anger, reluctance to discuss war experiences, interpersonal distance from loved ones, a tendency to stay at home and avoid socializing, and reluctance to seek help for destructive reactions they accepted as normal in a combat zone. These residual inclinations are usually unconscious but often become a lifestyle and then necessitate extensive treatment over many years.

Our female veterans can have additional stress from either overt abuse or the threat of abuse in a combat zone. That threat is an obvious concern if captured by the enemy but is equally destructive if it comes from "friendly" troops. Once abused or threatened with abuse from "friendly" comrades, women warriors often have to live with the risk of a repeat encounter. To report the problem may only raise questions that are hard to prove and can end up making the accuser the victim. Reporting the incident is still the right thing to do, but these threatened women may have to live in daily contact with "not-so-friendly" comrades. The constant reminder of her vulnerability is an additional corrosive stress a female veteran may experience in a combat zone. It is necessary that we learn the value of working through combat zone stresses for *both* women and men before they return from combat duty.

So, what's the answer to resolve War-Damage for most combat veterans on their way home? It's my recommendation that we spend the funds necessary to establish "Welcome Home Compounds" in remote island/beach areas such as Guam or Hawaii. Our veterans would stop there for three weeks on their way home as a part of their normal combat rotation. Ideally, we should take the three weeks from the end of their tour and make the *welcome home time* part of their normal rotation.

Why three weeks? That knowledge comes from <u>experience in Hospital Admissions for Stress Reduction</u>. A one week stay is usually ineffective. Two weeks of attention is a start but does not allow enough decompression or relief for effective stress reduction. Three weeks is normally sufficient to help reduce stress and allow healing to begin. Three weeks with veterans will also allow options such as having loved ones join them the last week for a better transition returning home. It's certainly rewarding to have veterans who are long-absent father's or mother's come home to needy children. It may be even more so to see a mother and father come home arm-in-arm together.

Such compounds can be basic but need to be private and away from the public.

These welcome home settings need to be appealing, and need to include civilian comforts, such as long distance phone access, private rooms with en-suite bathrooms, king-size beds, sitting areas to read, and televisions with Skype access so veterans can interact visually with loved ones back home.

With their efficient construction methods, the Seabees could build or supervise private contractors to build these compounds in a few months. Compounds should include attractive dining facilities, administrative quarters, gym facilities, medical facilities, movie theaters, beach huts and recreational gear to play tennis, golf, sail boats, swim, etc. The Seabees already have equipment and trained personnel. With a suitable location and naval ships to deliver personnel, materials, and equipment, entire compounds could be built quickly at reasonable costs. By building offshore with military equipment and personnel, it might be possible to save the expense of hiring, transporting, and housing expensive labor. The politicians could get some credit by negotiating with home unions to help build at reduced fees. In addition to "America First," it is time to make *"Veterans First!"*

We would obviously need male and female accommodations in a relaxing place where veterans could independently enjoy time in the sun, scuba diving, snorkeling, sailing, and relaxing on the beach. Male and female compounds could be adjacent, since adult vets will make their own decisions about socialization. Local chefs and staff should serve them meals as in a gracious hotel. With basics like hot water, good lighting, and no military chores, the veterans wouldn't be on duty or have cleaning details, KP, or other military duties. They could shape up their rooms as they like, but they'd be considered honored guests instead of active combat soldiers.

We could train and use a *Combat Veterans Corps* instead of expensive professionals as group facilitators to act as mentors during daily group meetings. Each group would be comprised of a specific group of six to eight vets (both female and male) starting their three-week cycle together. Each group would normally stay together to discuss their tour during their time in Welcome Home.

In private practice, I spent thirty-five years doing group therapy with every level of mental health disturbance. With new patients, I'd spend the necessary time individually to understand their issues and build trust. As soon as possible, I introduced them to an existing group already in place and then met with new patients in the group instead of individual therapy. The Group approach was more effective and worked more quickly that one-on-one treatment.

It would be easy to train a Corps of combat veterans (CVC) to sit, listen, and encourage returning veterans to discuss their war experiences. We could have several dozen CVC mentors available and ready to serve after a few weeks of training. We could hire them on a simple retainer and pay their transport and expenses to serve in the Welcome Home Compounds with a set group rotating through their three week stay. We have many available military psychiatrists and psychologists in the Marines, Navy, Army, and Air Force that could easily train combat veterans as welcome home facilitators in a short period of time. Combat Veterans Corps' (CVC) facilitators do not need prolonged training in order to fix, diagnose or treat PTSD War-Damage. Their military status and combat experience are their credentials. All they need *is their been there background* and caring attitude to get the vets talking.

The home-bound combat veterans will respond to a combat facilitator who has been there. Both female and male CVC personnel will understand the stress and trauma combat vets have experienced. They've been through the confusing, automatic, and disruptive personal reactions while transitioning from an active combat zone combat to the needs of a sedate home-life. The basic requirement of such facilitators is to care and listen in a relaxed, decompressed environment.

There is little need for the facilitator to make insightful judgments or tell the veterans what to do. Veterans who survived combat, they have what it takes to overcome War-Damage, as long as they understand it and deal with the CSS automatics before returning home. Most returning veterans (male or female) have little awareness they're not the same person who left home to go to war. It's unfair to ask them to naively wait until their lives are in turmoil to find out they've changed while serving in a combat zone and need insight and personal control to adjust back home.

It will be important to have both female and male facilitators work together to start and depart with each three-week group. *Women are inherently more sensitive, instinctive, caring, forgiving, and protective than men.* Their ability to conceive, birth, and nurture a helpless child who is totally dependent on a mother's attention and support is the only skill set women need to understand War-Damaged vets. Having a caring woman as one of the facilitators will encourage veterans to more comfortably share difficult memories of War-Damage trauma. After hundreds of hours of working with therapy groups, I've confirmed the positive impact women have on suffering patients struggling to recall and resolve past trauma.

The CVC (Combat Veterans Corps) male and female facilitators would obviously need some income for their valuable contribution. Even so, they wouldn't be nearly as expensive as Ph.D. psychologists or MD psychiatrists working in a hospital setting. They could also be available as support for the veteran's family for several months when the veteran returns to the "world." Follow-up is rarely available now in the overworked VA system.

Mentors from the CVC could be on call for the veteran, his wife, and loved ones by phone. The CVC's bonding with the veteran and loved ones during the three-week Welcome Home discussions would make it possible for the familiar facilitator to talk through transition problems by phone and decompress crisis events causing upheaval. The advantage of the facilitators being on call is that most veterans don't have ongoing access to someone they know and who knows them for follow-up. It's important to have a combat veteran available who may have experienced similar upset or adjustment problems after returning home.

The facilitators could also be a resource for professionals working with veterans who need additional support after coming home. This available real-time support from a familiar mentor will be much more efficient and effective than years of intermittent contact and associated medications trying to help resolve mental health problems of PTSD. That misunderstood mental health label is now needed to get financial support for insurance coverage, but that requirement completes the chronic cycle of "mislabeled War-Damage." A PTSD diagnosis and sporadic contact with an overworked bureaucracy, dependent on medications, is well intended but not the right answer.

My brother (a helicopter crew chief with the Army in Vietnam) points out how important "on-call" support is for wives with children. A loving wife may have great patience with an explosive combat vet, but, if he scares her children or hurts her, she's still a mother and all bets are off. A single slap in anger scares a gentle wife or small child and can easily lead to separation or divorce.

A timely call by the wife to the familiar *welcome home facilitator* allows a chance to talk things through and help calm the situation. The facilitator may then ask to speak to the veteran and talk straight with him. The camaraderie felt by the vet may give an opportunity to work through acute upset. That constructive pause to calm things down, correct the veteran's behavior, and/or get an apology could save both the veteran and his marriage. Facilitators would need access to backup from on-call professionals to help in desperate situations, but this could be set up with existing civilian professionals.

Another strong support asset may be the existing spouse support groups commonly formed by those who have loved ones at sea or serving overseas. Men and women from those support groups could be incorporated into constructive contact with the mentors of the CVC. Those known support persons may be a more comfortable first contact when things go wrong with a returning vet.

Members of those support groups often have a relationship with the upset spouse and are therefore more likely to lend a sympathetic ear. Any asset or help we can have available to facilitate a constructive outcome for *flashes of turmoil* are worth exploring. We need to use every opportunity to minimize the War-Damage that leads to the long-term symptoms of PTSD and the prolonged treatment we now find so necessary.

Continuing support is crucial for the successful resolution of unresolved PTSD that veterans experience returning from a war zone. Little support is now provided unless a veteran can wait for an additional appointment at the Veteran's Administration. That may take weeks or months of time and be too late to avoid destruction of a marriage or a possible *"self-rescue response"* (my term) for acute suicidal decisions.

Getting timely attention to vets on their way home is only part of the War-Damage solution. Loved ones and relatives need exposure to their vets' combat trauma and without knowledge of the corrosive impact and necessary personality changes (combat survival skills, CSS) their vet brings home, spouses, siblings, and parents are easily blindsided by War-Damage reactions. It would therefore be important to have a spouse, parent, adult sibling, or close relative come to the Welcome Home Compound the last few days of the veteran's three-week stay. They could meet the facilitator and reestablish contact with veterans in a relaxed, island atmosphere. If the home folks were flown on military transports, it could be relatively inexpensive and let us return the veteran home with their loved ones on the same transport without additional expense.

The loved one would attend the regular combat discussion meetings with their vet for about four days. The first couple of days the vets would set at their usual place in the group circle and continue their group discussion. The loved one would set directly behind their vet and be instructed not to talk, laugh, or make any comments while the group continued their ongoing discussion of combat experiences. The facilitator would encourage each vet to contribute during the session. The discussion of combat trauma would be relatively candid since the veterans have already been talking and could not see or hear any reactions from their own love one.

About the third session, seats would be reversed, and the vet would sit directly behind their loved one with instructions to be silent and nonreactive to comments, questions, or discussion from anyone while the loved one's talked. The facilitator would have the front circle of loved ones share what they had learned from the veterans' discussions about combat duty in a war zone and the associated stress a veteran might have encountered.

The closing group session about day four would have individual veterans and their loved ones talk only to each other as the rest of the group listened without comment. Each pair of vets and their loved one would then together share with the facilitator what they'd learned about each other's lives while they were apart. The structured process of *"Exposure Discussion"* would help vets and loved ones be in tune to each other's fears, needs, and reactions when they returned to the World after completing the three weeks of Welcome Home.

The idea of a Welcome Home Compound in a pleasant setting should be well received once veterans are on a USA island that is prepared and honored to see them coming home. If the stopover were included as part of their normal rotation home, they'd quickly value the understanding and adjustment they could make returning from a combat zone to their loved ones. Spouses, family, and loved ones would find the returning veteran decompressed, calmer, and with much better insight regarding his/her lingering War-Damage.

Ideally, the availability of such a program would be introduced as part of advanced training in preparation for soldiers assigned to a combat zone. A CVC representative could discuss the support available as part of their combat deployment. The three weeks in a pleasant Welcome Home Compound could then become a constructive ending to their combat deployment rather than just a delay returning home.

I'm not aware that we've ever tried this approach before, but it's most enlightening to remember that combat veterans returning during World War II were on ships for weeks at a time. They were allowed to relax, goof off, sunbathe, and talk to each other. That wasn't the total adjustment needed, compared to this "welcome home" concept but, nevertheless, the weeks of talking onboard ships of returning World War II veterans was helpful for decompression and discussion therapy.

In my experience dealing with hundreds of psychological casualties in Vietnam, I became firmly convinced that the Officers and NCOs referring stress casualties were far better than I was at identifying Marines who needed help. Those same individuals would be invaluable working with returning veterans in relaxed Welcome Home Compounds. We spend millions of dollars and months of time preparing each soldier for their combat duties. They are intensely trained to kill, work as a unit, and care for each other. We spend millions more paying them and supporting their duties and missions in a combat zone. Our nation needs to consider giving our troops the opportunity for a *welcome home* experience that will help them decompress and limit the impact of War-Damage that may disrupt their return to civilian life. They've served our country well, and we owe this "welcome home" adjustment to returning veterans who have fought and given so much for their country.

Having been there and experienced War-Damage and CSS firsthand, I feel strongly that this approach will work. We could always start with a prototype compound and document the value of providing help on the way home versus the disorienting, "deep end of the pool" approach we now use to bring War-Damaged vets, back to the world.

Only after years of disruptive PTSD symptoms do I know what it means to be loved, approved, and accepted by my loving wife of thirty-five years. Without her, I may not have survived my occasional suicidal ideation. Keep in mind that it's often the strong ones who commit suicide, not the weak or those needing to hurt someone. I was taught that myth about suicide being by the weak during my training in the 1960s. I now know it takes a lot of courage to put a gun to your head. Combat veterans have such courage, and when all hope is gone, they may resort to a "self-rescue" that is unnecessarily final and devastating to those they leave behind.

Nevertheless, "self-rescue" (suicide) may be an understandable (but preventable) reaction for the prolonged problems some veterans experience and the destructive lives they face trying to get back to *peace and purpose* in their civilian world.

This approach will take the support and commitment of our government leaders. Let's take care of our brave women and men returning from war this time, rather than leave them with the War Damage we exposed them to in order to protect and meet the needs of our country.

Let's welcome them home!

Respectfully Recommended,

Ted D. Kilpatrick, Ph.D.
Former Lieutenant USNR
3RD Marine Division 1966 --1967

About the Author

Service with the Navy and Marine Corps started in the fall of 1965 when I received a direct commission as a USNR Naval Officer in the Medical Service Corps. I was assigned to Bethesda Naval Hospital in Washington DC for three months of Officer training in Naval procedures and how to serve in a military hospital.

My first duty station after training was as the Staff Psychologist at the Norfolk Naval Hospital in Norfolk, Virginia. I worked as a Psychologist and saw active duty personnel and dependents. In the early fall of 1966, I received orders to report as a Psychologist to the Third Marine Division in South Vietnam. The orders required 30 days at Camp Pendleton in California for Marine Corps combat training before going to Vietnam.

At Camp Pendleton I was in a squad of 12 medical officers also on their way to Vietnam. We learned to how clean, load and shoot M-14 rifles and 45 caliber pistols. We marched at night through hills with hidden spider holes where Marines shot blanks in our direction if we missed recognizing the danger. The veteran gunny sergeant had a difficult group of unhappy "DOCs" to teach necessary combat survival skills. We complained of the long hours and hard nighttime demands. Once in the combat zone the value of this intense exposure to combat realities became obvious and much appreciated.

I arrived in Da Nang, South Vietnam for duty as Division Psychologist of the Third Marine Division and was there several weeks before moving to the Third Marine Division Field Hospital in Phu Bai South Vietnam. The field hospital was in Division Headquarters located 10 miles SE of Hue in northern South Vietnam near the DMZ (Demilitarized Zone) and North Vietnam.

In 1966 and 1967 there was intense fighting surrounding our compound. Night mortar attacks and probes at the security wires were common.

The Marines built a ten-cot screened hut to house psychological causalities who were not also physically wounded. If the fighting was spaced over several days and I had cot room, I had a chance to treat damaged Marines in country. When hit hard with numerous causalities I had to evacuate psychological casualties to the hospital ships, Japan or back to the USA.

Upon leaving Vietnam in the fall of 1967 I received orders to report as the Staff Psychologist at the Naval Hospital in Jacksonville, Florida. This provided an opportunity to work with a few of the Marines I had had to evacuate directly from combat. They did not recover as well as those I was able to see in country but quickly warmed to me and trusted me when they found out I was a combat veteran.

I left the Navy at the end of my three-year commitment and went on to complete my Ph.D. at the University of Florida starting in1969. My degree in Clinical Psychology and the required internship was finished in December 1971. I had an individual private practice in Jacksonville, Florida the next 43 years working as both a clinical and industrial psychologist. I took a 10-year time in mid 1994out to work as an executive with Gate Petroleum in construction and manufacturing. This broadened my knowledge of business, finance and investing.

I retain my Florida Psychology License and still see a few veterans returning from Mideast combat pro bono. Their suicide rate is very high, and they hate to seek help so escape through drugs and alcohol is too common. Once self-respect, purpose and value are gone, suicide becomes an attractive "self-rescue" response.

The purpose of this book is to confirm that residual combat war-damage is not a mental illness. CSS (combat survival skills) that veterans come home with need patient understanding, relieving/in-depth disclosure and soul-caring acceptance such as that available from gentle women and trained dogs.

Endnotes

1. https://www.ptsd.va.gov/The Vietnam Helicopter Pilots Association

2. Veteran Affairs Office

3. Veterans Administration

4. Department of Veteran Affairs

5. National Center for PTSD

6. A Guide for Military Personnel

7. A Guide for Families of Military Members (Home Coming)

8. The Walter Reed Army Institute of Research (WRAIR)

9. U.S. Army Medical Research and Material Command Division

10. JAMA Psychiatry. 2015 Nov;72(11):1127-34. doi: 10.1001/ jamapsychiatry.2015.1786.

Made in the USA
San Bernardino, CA
25 February 2020

64937293R00066